D0969415

Get Your Ducks in a Row

480 Simple Ideas to Organize Your House and Your Life

Rosalie Nourse

Trafford rev. 10/26/2012

 www.trafford.com

North America & international
toll-free: 1 888 232 4444 (USA & Canada)
phone: 250 383 6864 ♦ fax: 812 355 4082

To my husband

—my best friend, devoted fan and ardent cheerleader,
for your unwavering love and support in everything I pursue

To my children

—being your mom is the best career I ever loved.
You inspire me by engaging life with energy, strength and courage.

For Bryson, Ellie, Quincy, Johnny and Charly

"All your dreams can come true if you have the courage to pursue them."

Walt Disney

Lest you think I'm perfectly organized, please know that I still misplace my car keys on a regular basis.

Rosalie

Contents

Author's Note

Are you ready to get organized? Are you geared up to get rid of the clutter on your desktop? When was the last time you misplaced your cell phone or car keys? Are you running out the door late for another appointment? That's where this book comes in. By the time you finish reading, you'll have 480 helpful tips and ideas to organize your house and your life.

Before you begin reading, however, take a minute and answer these two questions:

o   Why did you buy this book?
o   What do you hope to gain from the ideas presented?

The definition of "organized" is "to be systematic or to give structure." The definition of disorganized is "functioning without adequate order." Clutter defined is "a disorderly heap." One person's idea of being organized could be totally different from another's. One person's idea of "clutter' is someone else's idea of treasures, things to keep and/or cherish.

Whatever your idea of being organized is, there's one thing that's important. After you spend the time getting the rooms of your house orderly you need a compelling reason why you'd want your house to stay that way. Without the desire and behavior to maintain orderliness, you may as well just open the phone book and call one of these professional organizers. Someone will come to your house, help you sort through your belongings and help you decide what to keep and what to toss. She will help you find a place for your remaining items. When she leaves, your house will look like a model home out of a decorating magazine and you'll have paid a small fortune for its appearance. However, if you don't have a compelling reason to keep it that way on a daily basis, your house will quickly become a mess again. Your hard earned money for the professional help just went down the drain and you're back where you started. Yikes!

Personally speaking, when there's clutter around me, or I can't find what I'm looking for, it stresses me. Because of the stress I strive to keep the rooms of my house in order. When someone opens a cupboard, the contents are neatly arranged, most of the time anyway. I want to find what I need when I need it. I don't want to waste time and energy looking for misplaced eyeglasses or car keys before I leave the house. The stress is not worth it.

What are your reasons for desiring a de-cluttered house or managing your time efficiently? Will an orderly house give you more time to spend with your family? Would it cut out unnecessary time spent looking for misplaced items? Would managing your time effectively make you feel more peaceful and in harmony with yourself? A well-organized house can increase the quality of your life. It's time to get your ducks in a row!

Rosalie

Tools for Organizing

Life is so much better when everything in the house has its own place. To get organized you'll need tools of all kinds. Here are some ideas to get you started.

Bins, baskets, crates and trays are staples for organizing all that you have. They come in various sizes with covers or not. These must-have containers are made of plastic, wood, woven wicker, canvas, glass, metal and other materials and come in all colors. Containers can be decorative and colorful to keep out in the open or made of plastic to conceal behind closed doors. Lined woven baskets are classic. Square and rectangular shapes make the most efficient use of space. Wicker baskets with cotton liners are inexpensive and versatile. Plastic storage bins are cheap and on sale throughout the year.

Storage bins are the mainstay in any home's organizing system. They are sturdier than cardboard boxes. Moisture doesn't damage them and mice can't get into them. You can see the contents inside clear ones. Only purchase storage bins with sturdy lids that latch. They are easy to open and close and the lid doesn't accidentally come off spewing contents everywhere. Storage bins come in all dimensions from shoebox size to gallon size. Each home can easily use several dozen. For garage storage you'll need even more.

Whether you're using baskets or bins, strategically place storage containers everywhere—think in terms of above, below or on top of shelves, tables, wall units and other furniture in your house.

Deck boxes are the ideal solution for organizing just about everything used outdoors. They're ample in size with lids that keep the water out. Some can double as benches. Purchase them for less at pre-summer or end of summer clearance sales.

Drawer organizers and dividers help maximize the storage space in every drawer. Similar items are separated from other items making it easier to find what you need.

Microfiber towels hold 7 times their weight in water. They dry items faster than regular cotton towels. They won't scratch and can be used on all types of materials including your car. They are especially useful in the kitchen for drying items you wash by hand.

Spiral notebooks are not just for school kids. Buy them in multiples in different sizes and colors whenever school supplies go on sale. Notebooks keep information all in one place. It's easy to flip through the pages for what you need instead of looking for loose pieces of paper or sticky notes.

Shelves can be hung most anywhere. They are available in all styles, materials, widths and lengths. Use them for displaying books, collectibles, decorative figurines or photo frames in bathrooms, bedrooms, the living room, dining room, utility room and family rooms. Do you have a spare bedroom that doubles as an office or craft room? Add shelves to the closet. Use the shelves for small bins filled with craft items, for books, to layer sewing fabric or for storing sewing and ironing supplies. Hang a shelf above your office desk to house 3 ring binders. Look up to find more storage space. Shelves can be hung over doorways and windows. A floor to ceiling shelving unit can corral multiple accessories. Install shelves in cabinets without a second shelf to make efficient use of space.

Magazine holders are specially designed for storing full size magazines in an upright position. Purchase them inexpensively in office supply stores. Holders reduce the clutter and help you locate magazines when needed.

PART ONE
Organize your House

Backyard—your family's outdoor room

Your outdoor dining experience and playing in the back yard with your kids or guests can be relaxing and enjoyable when the needed supplies are neatly organized and within easy reach.

1 A deck box on the patio with a built in bench back can store the large outdoor furniture cushions and pillows during rainy days.

2 A separate deck box closer to the outdoor dining table can hold four to six chair cushions.

3 What about the huge assortment of kids' outdoor toys? A deck box is large enough to hold a bucket of baseballs, bats, bases and mitts, playground balls, soccer balls, badminton racquets and the croquet set.

4 Not all cities and counties provide recycling containers. Make your own recycling center using a large covered deck box. Place two large plastic bins inside the deck box as dividers. Glass and aluminum go on one side, newspapers on the other. Lift boxes to curb or take to recycling center when bins are full. Situate the deck box just inside the garage door if you have an attached garage. Otherwise, place the bin on the deck just outside your back door. If it's in a handy location, it's easier to immediately carry recyclable containers from the kitchen to the box.

5 Storage bins with secure clamp down lids, 22 gallons and larger, are perfect containers to house everything you need for outdoor dining. Unlike cardboard boxes that can fall apart, plastic bins are sturdy. Lids stay tightly closed keeping contents virtually dust-free.

6 Designate one large storage bin with what you'll need to set the table outdoors. You can also be kind to the environment by eliminating the use of paper and one-use plastic cutlery when dining outside. Plates, bowls and tumblers such as ones by Tupperware are unbreakable and reusable. Purchase an inexpensive set of metal flatware. Store everything outdoors near the dining table in a plastic covered bin. Contents stay dry even in the rain. You can easily set the table for meals and only need to bring the food out.

7 When you're eating outdoors why not make the dining experience as nice as if you were dining indoors? Set the table with cloth table linens or cloth placemats and napkins, all neatly stored in a storage bin with a latching lid. Cloth table linens are reusable and kinder to the environment. After dining, carry linens or placemats inside to be washed. Return items to the bin afterwards so they're available when you need them.

8 For more elegant dining, consider repurposing one of your dinnerware sets for the outdoors. If you have a screened house, a covered patio or an outdoor kitchen, dinnerware can easily be stored in a waterproof outdoor cabinet or in a separate covered plastic bin with a lid. Include beverage glasses in your outdoor storage bin. Acrylic tumblers look as nice as glass ones but are unbreakable. They are heavier than paper products with less chance of being blown over by the wind. When stored in a covered bin, contents stay dry and mostly dust-free. You'll avoid the hassle of bringing tableware outside for every meal thus saving you time.

9 Designate another covered storage bin to hold items you use frequently outdoors such as citronella candles, spare votive candles for outdoor lanterns, butane lighter, outdoor candles or LED candles or a bucket of kindling for starting a fire. Store the bin on the patio or deck so it's easily within reach.

10 Did it rain and now your table and plastic chairs are wet or dirty from particles thrown around by the wind? Keep a roll or two of paper towels and a spray bottle of all-purpose cleaner nearby for washing them down before use. You'll avoid having to run inside for cleaning supplies. Store these items in the same bin with linens or tableware.

11 Keep several large serving trays with handles in the kitchen pantry or utility room for carrying food entrees from the house to the patio table. These trays are also helpful to bring dirty dishes back to the house.

Car—your residence and office away from home

Between your own personal errands, commuting for work appointments and the kids' school and extracurricular activities, some days you may think you live in your car. Carry things in the car that you may need for yourself and the kids. A system to keep your vehicle clean and organized is a must.

12 Divide your CD's between the areas you use them—the CD player in the car and the player in the house. Rotate the CD's periodically to vary your musical entertainment. Many styles of CD cases are available—ones that clip to the car visor so you can keep your favorite CD's handy or cases that hold dozens of CD's without the CD hard case. Catalog the CD's by artist or genre so you can easily find the perfect one every time.

13 If you frequently consume hot drinks while on the go, be kind to the environment and buy a reusable commuter mug to reduce paper cup usage. You'll want your commuter mug to be of sturdy material with a spill-proof lid. Some espresso shops will reward your eco-friendly style by giving you a discount when you use your personal cup for your favorite drink.

14 Purchase 2 reusable commuter mugs. Inevitably, one will be in the dishwasher or dirty on the kitchen counter when you want it for the car. When it comes out of the dishwasher, immediately place it in your car tote so you'll have it in the car for your next coffee shop visit.

15 Buy several good quality reusable water bottles to take with you in the car. Test to see that the bottles are liquid tight. Nothing is worse than having your water bottle leak into your purse, car tote or gym bag.

16 Fill your insulated, reusable water bottle with ice cubes and water before you leave the house so you'll have cold drinking water handy while you're out doing errands, driving to work or taking your turn with the car pool.

17 When you're back in the house, put your water bottle on the kitchen counter so it can go in the dishwasher with the day's dirty dishes.

18 Save time and money by developing the habit of refilling your bottles with water when they come out of the dishwasher, then place them in the refrigerator. You'll always have a fresh bottle to grab as you head out the door.

19 When you stop for gas, take your personal water bottle or commuter container inside the store. You can refill your container with ice and water for free. You'll by-pass the long line at the counter of folks making beverage purchases and you'll save the expense of bottled water.

20 When you're out and about and want a cold drink such as a soda or iced tea, stop at a gas station or convenience store. Take your commuter container inside and fill it with your preferred beverage at the do-it-yourself fountain. At the check-out counter, show your container and ask for the" refill price." Most gas stations will honor your request or give your refill beverage to you for free with gas purchase.

21 Hang a trash bag anywhere you can in your car. A plastic grocery shopping bag works well because it has handles to hang it and holds an ample amount of trash. Put all trash in there and empty it frequently. Nothing looks worse than paper wrappers and other litter strewn about the car seats and floor.

22 If you allow your children to eat in the car, ask them to hand you their food wrappers, paper cups and straws when they're done eating. You can place them in the car trash bag immediately and save having to go around checking for refuse later.

23 Buy a large, washable, sturdy tote bag that is non-collapsible and has handles. This is the bag you take in the car with you every time you leave the house. It keeps frequently used items readily available in your car without loading down your purse. It should be large enough to carry these items:

- Reusable water bottle filled with cold drinking water
- Unbreakable commuter mug in case you decide to stop for a beverage
- A pencil case with office supplies (pencil, pen, calculator, note pad, highlighter)
- Individually wrapped anti-bacterial wipes to sanitize restaurant or coffee shop tables
- Electronic tablet, day planner or notebook that contains your To Do list
- Items for your errands: books to the library, letters to mail, etc.
- An insulated lunch bag with snacks for you and/or the kids if you plan to be gone for several hours

24 If you have an in-home business, carry your product catalogs, product samples and marketing materials in a tote bag and take it with you every time you leave home. You always want to be prepared to conduct business whenever the opportunity arises.

25 Designate specific tote bags for each regularly scheduled activity on your family calendar:

- Workout clothes for the fitness center
- Bible, lesson sheets, pen and notebook for bible study class
- The necessary gear for each family member's sport
- Craft supplies for next meeting

On the day of the activity, place the appropriate bag by the door you'll exit. When not in use, hang the bags in bedroom or office closets to easily grab.

26 Every time you arrive home, clear the car of whatever doesn't permanently belong there:

- Pick up all trash that may have landed on the car floor and deposit it in the garage wastebasket.
- Gather up all beverage containers from all cup holders.
- Put purchases and all miscellaneous papers in your tote bag to carry into the house.

27 Keep an extra shopping bag in your car for removing items that are too bulky to put in your regular tote bag. After emptying the contents in their proper place in the house, place the shopping bag by the exit door so you can take it back to the car on your next trip.

28 Store pump bottles of anti-bacterial hand cleanser in each vehicle. An 8 oz. bottle conveniently fits in the door compartment. When you're back in the car from the grocery store or your activity, create a habit of cleansing your hands. Pass the hand cleanser around to your spouse and kids so they can do the same.

29 Maintain a mini-personal care kit in the glove box of the car you use most. Items could include:

- Small hair brush
- Travel size hair spray
- Small tube of hand lotion
- Wet wipes
- Pack of tissues
- Paper napkins
- Extra plastic forks and spoons from carry-out restaurants in their original plastic wrap

30 Keep a stash of your favorite trail mix or granola bars in your car in airtight containers. These are quick and healthy snacks when hunger hits you. You won't need to stop at the store or be tempted by high-calorie snacks at the gas station. In addition, you'll save money.

31 In winter, keep emergency supplies in your car in a closed container:

- Lightweight fleece blanket or emergency blanket
- Large candle in a tin
- Matches in a small airtight container
- Extra pairs of gloves and mittens
- Power bars and trail mix
- Bottled water

32 If you live in snow country or a rural area, make it a rule to accessorize your car with what you might need in the winter to walk a mile or two in inclement weather if need be:

- Warm fleece pants
- Snow boots
- Wool socks
- Warm hat and neck scarf
- Fleece pullover or cardigan to wear under your coat

33 Line your car trunk or the rear of your SUV with a sturdy, washable blanket. It helps keep your vehicle clean and can be used to keep warm in an emergency. It's also handy for an impromptu picnic or to sit on at a sporting event.

34 Car organizers with numerous pockets of different sizes can be sewn from a pattern or purchased pre-made. They hold road maps, notepad and pencils/pens, magazine, snacks, small toys, water bottle, hand lotion, hand sanitizer and other useful car items.

35 Have you ever accidentally locked your keys in the car? You can save yourself and family members a lot of time and stress by purchasing a car entry key from your dealership. An entry key is anti-theft since the key only opens the car door.

One needs an ignition key to start the car. Put the entry key in a sturdy metal key box with a strong magnet. Attach the key box to the undercarriage of your car. You'll never have to call a locksmith again or wait for a family member to arrive with spare keys. Buy entry keys for each vehicle you own.

36 Keep a spare pair of inexpensive sunglasses in the car for those times when you forgot yours at home.

37 Unexpectedly caught in a downpour? With an umbrella in your car, you'll stay dry. It will store neatly and out of the way in the pouch on the back of the driver's or passenger's seat.

38 Every car needs a container to corral the loose stuff that you need while doing errands. A plastic shoebox size container without a lid works well for this. Place it on the front seat within easy reach or between the front seats if space allows. It keeps items from being all over the car and can hold supplies such as:

- A mileage notebook
- Small spiral notebook
- Pens for writing and for recording miles driven, if needed, for tax purposes
- Small flashlight
- Snacks, like trail mix, in a small container with a seal
- Your sunglasses for when the sun ducks behind the clouds

39 Use felt tipped pens for your mileage notebook or for writing other notes in the car. Ball point pens won't write in cold weather or when held in an upright position. Keep several on hand.

40 When new phone books are delivered to your house, oftentimes the package includes a smaller version of the phone book with business contacts only. Keep that phone book in the car. If you don't have a smartphone with internet access, you can still look up business contacts, addresses and phone numbers from the book when away from home.

Children's Bedrooms—a place of their own

Children need a place to store their personal belongings and find the daily clothes they need. If it's well organized you can teach them to keep the room neat and tidy.

41 Chests of drawers utilize valuable floor space in a bedroom. Instead, use wire slide out basket systems for children's clothing. You can build the system with the number of baskets desired.

42 Whether you use drawer chests or a wire basket system for children's clothing, place it in the bedroom closet for maximum space efficiency. Remove the closet doors for easy access to clothing.

43 Label each basket or drawer—pajamas, underwear, socks, jeans, other pants, sports clothing (shin guards, soccer shorts, soccer socks, etc.). It's easy for children to find their clothes each day and to put clean clothes away.

44 Hang all children's clothing—dresses, shirts, tops and t-shirts on hangers. Hangers make it easier for children to find clothes instead of rummaging through piles of items in a basket or drawer. Place the hangers on a clothing rod above the wire basket systems/drawer chest. Hang the clothing rod within easy reach of a child or provide a small stable step stool in the closet for child's use.

45 Place a tall wicker clothes hamper with a lid for dirty clothes in each child's room. Teach your child to toss dirty clothes into the hamper each night before donning pajamas or taking a shower or bath. The hamper helps keep the room clean and is easy to carry to the laundry room.

46 Purchase a tall, unfinished bookcase for each child's room. A five shelf bookcase is most useful. Paint or stain the bookcase to match the child's room color. For maximum safety, secure the bookcase to the wall with strong bolts The bookcase is home for treasures such as a piggy bank, collectible items and the child's favorite toys.

47 Buy a tall, unfinished, hanging book rack for your child's room. A book rack with four sections will work best. Paint or stain the bookcase to match the child's room. Secure it to the wall with strong bolts. With a hanging book rack you can save on floor space giving the child more room to play. The bookrack will hold dozens of books for bedtime or any-time reading.

48 Store the bulk of a child's book collection on a closet shelf above the clothing rod. Periodically rotate these books with the ones in the hanging book rack.

49 Provide a clock radio for your child's bedside table. Set the radio so music will play when it's time for the child to get up for school. Teach your child to be self-reliant and responsible by arising when the music begins to play.

50 By the time a child starts school, she needs a desk as a regular place to complete homework and prepare school projects. Even a small one with a few drawers will work. It can fit in a corner of her room. Fill the drawers with pencils, an eraser, stapler and crayons. Hang a bulletin board above the desk so your child can display her artwork and school papers.

51 Teaching a child to make his bed saves you time and energy and teaches the child to be responsible. Keep bed coverings simple—a set of sheets, a blanket and comforter or a duvet cover plus a couple pillows. Neatness will come later. For now be content that he pulls up the covers and makes a good effort at making the bed.

Children's Playroom—where imaginations come alive

By the time children are toddlers, it's helpful to have a designated place other than their bedroom to keep their toys or to work with crafts. You could section off a corner of the basement or family room if you don't have the luxury of a spare bedroom to use as a playroom.

52 Stock the playroom with these supplies:

- a table at a child's seating level with 2-4 chairs
- a tall wall unit with shelves
- labeled baskets to hold building blocks, small dolls, Lincoln logs, trains and tracks and other toys with multiple parts
- recycled computer paper and drawing pads for artwork
- a roll of white butcher paper for large art projects
- craft supplies: washable crayons and felt markers, watercolor paint sets, finger paint sets, pencils and erasers, scotch tape dispenser, a stapler, blunt paper scissors
- a dry erase floor easel with dry erase markers and an eraser for drawing
- play kitchen with dish sets

53 If the playroom is a spare bedroom, remove the closet doors. Place a chest of drawers inside the closet for storing play things such as dress up clothes, card games, dominoes, board games and puzzles. Use the closet's top shelf for larger games and puzzles.

54 Install a tall, five shelf book case in the playroom to hold toys. To save money, buy an unfinished one, then paint or stain it to match room décor. Secure the book case to the wall with strong bolts. Place wicker or plastic baskets on the shelves to corral loose toys such as Legos, Lincoln Logs, train sets and building blocks. Label the baskets. When it's time to put the toys away, all sets have a home.

55 Tired of finding your child's crayons and felt markers all over the house? Store them in the playroom in individual metal buckets. Mount the buckets on drawer pulls hung above the playroom table. The bucket is easily removed. You could put the bucket in a tote bag with a pad of paper and conveniently cart it to a restaurant to keep children occupied before the meal is served.

56 Do you have hundreds of dollars invested in your child's Lego sets? Legos are an educational, recreational and collectible expenditure. Help your child care for them as well as find the exact pieces they need for their building projects. Lego now sells specific containers with divided sections for easy storage of all those tiny bits and pieces. As an alternative, check out the men's tool department for other sturdy sectioned containers with a secure lid and strong handles. These are the containers enthusiasts use to store their valuable hardware. You'll need 3-4 or more depending on your child's growing collection.

57 When you're vacuuming the house do you sometimes come across a stray Lego piece on the floor and are tempted to just let the vacuum suck it up? Stop! You or a loved one paid for that Lego piece, no matter how small. Pick it up by hand and for now, toss it in the kitchen junk drawer. It can be retrieved and placed in its proper place later.

58 Want some inexpensive containers for your child's toys? The next time you're at your local ice cream store, ask for the large empty ice cream containers. They're free. They can be wrapped in decorative contact paper, if desired, then labeled. Use these bins for toys of all kinds—wooden building blocks, Lincoln Logs, wooden train sets, small dolls. When it's time to pick up toys, the children will know where each toy belongs.

59 You don't need fancy bookcases or shelves to store children's toys. The free ice cream containers from the store will suffice and can be placed on the bedroom or playroom floor. The important thing is to have a place to keep the toys organized and make clean-up time simpler.

60 With a place for every item, teach children to put away playthings when not in use.

61 Review the children's play area seasonally to discard broken toys or games and puzzles with missing pieces.

Garage—home for your vehicles

Next to your house, your vehicles are the biggest ticket items. They need to be protected from the elements. Make a decision that your garage is where you house your cars, your tools and a limited amount of storage in bins. The garage is neither a holding place for displaced items nor an overflowing storage area for stuff. Act on your decision by clearing out the clutter.

62 Cleaning out the garage can be a fun activity.

- Set aside a Saturday to do it
- Involve the whole family
- Start by bringing the large trashcans into the garage
- Toss out broken items and items you haven't used in a year or more
- Restore displaced items to their proper place or make a pile of items that need a home
- After a couple hours, take a break, have lunch or order pizza.

- Load the car with thrift store donations in boxes or large trash bags. Deliver the items the same day if possible.
- Store the items you want to keep in large bins with sturdy lids.

    o   Label the contents.
    o   Stack the bins in an orderly fashion.

63 When you've cleaned out the garage, it may appear neatly organized but it may still harbor items you think you need. Mark a date on your calendar every spring to once again scrutinize the contents of each bin and box. What didn't you use last year that you can toss this year? What memorabilia can you let go of this year? It may take a year or two but gradually your garage will only contain items you use or really want to keep.

64 If you want to have a garage sale, schedule it within two weeks of flushing out the unwanted items. Call the thrift store to pick up the remaining items on the first business day after your garage sale.

65 Want a really fun way to get rid of a TV, sofa, desk chair or other large item without hauling it to the thrift store? Cart it to the curb and post a sign on it that says FREE. You'll be delighted to see that the item disappears within a couple hours.

66 For smaller items that you want to give away, place them in cardboard boxes and place at the curb or the end of your driveway. Write FREE on the box in large letters. Do not place items in bins or containers that you want to keep. Folks will take the containers along with the freebies!

67 If you're a baby boomer, or at empty nest, why are you keeping bins and boxes of your personal memorabilia and collectibles? Do your adult children want these items after you're gone? If not, sell the items on Craigslist or eBay. Use the extra money for your next trip.

68 Milk crates, old or new, make great storage containers for basketballs and playground balls. Keep the crates in the garage but keep them in close proximity to the basketball hoop or area where kids play dodge ball or four square.

69 Give each family member his/her own space in the garage. This allows each to keep what they want and keep it away from the belongings of other family members. Each person is responsible for this space, whether messy or neat.

70 If the household is down to just you and your spouse, have an imaginary line to divide the garage in half. One side of the garage is for her belongings; the other side for his belongings. Having one's own space can often end the battle of what belongs to whom and where it should be kept.

71 At its simplest, a double car garage should store the following:

- Two vehicles
- Workbenches
- Storage bins
- Sporting equipment
- Motorcycle and bikes
- Tool chests
- Cleaning supplies for washing and waxing the vehicles
- Memorabilia
- Gardening tools
- A sturdy broom or shop vacuum

72 If you find that the garage isn't big enough to hold your cars, the bicycles, your tools, a workbench or two, your storage bins, the lawnmower and other items you believe to be essential, it's time to consider building or purchasing a shed for additional space. The time and expense will be worth having your belongings organized and not crowded in the garage.

73 Each adult needs his/her own workbench in a size suitable for each one's interests whether that be storing shop tools, a place for her cycling helmet and biking tools or gardening tools.

74 If multiple members of the household help wash and wax vehicles, give each his/her own bucket with sponges and drying cloths. He can find them when needed and not fret that someone else misplaced his bucket or lost his sponges.

75 Men usually have a large assortment of tools. How about assembling a small tool box for the adult female in your family? Her tool box could consist of:

- Hammer
- Nails and screws in assorted sizes
- Needle nose pliers
- Regular pliers
- Diagonal cutters
- Box cutter
- Screwdrivers, standard and Phillips
- Duct tape
- Electrical tape
- Exacto knife
- Other items as needed

76 When your teens head off to college, gift each with a tool box filled with essential items—hammer, nails of assorted sizes and various kinds of screwdrivers and pliers. This will put them on a life-long learning experience of assembling and fixing their own things. In the beginning, they'll quickly make friends when others need help repositioning bunk beds and assembling desks.

77 Place wastebaskets on both sides of the inside of your garage. Line them with plastic trash bags for easy disposal. Keep the wastebaskets within easy reach of each vehicle so you can empty your car of trash on a daily basis.

78 The garage, shed or basement is a good place to store seasonal decorations in large storage bins. You'll want separate bins for different holidays or seasons—spring, summer, fall, winter, Easter, Valentine's Day, St. Patrick's Day, and Halloween. You may need a dozen or more bins just for Christmas decorations. Neatly label the bins by season using a black permanent marker.

*H*all Closet—a place for coats and jackets

The front hall closet could easily be the messiest storage area in the house. Its purpose is as a place for coats and jackets that your family members wear on a regular basis. It oftentimes ends up being the catch-all spot for sporting goods, boxes of odds and ends, jackets and coats that are no longer worn, and a place to harbor an endless number of stray items. In addition, rarely is there room in it to hang guests' coats. Strive to restore the front hall closet to its intended use.

79 Completely empty the closet contents. Peruse the coats and jackets and discard ones no longer worn or outgrown by your family members.

80 On an annual basis, donate coats and jackets in wearable condition to Goodwill, Coats for Kids or another non-profit organization.

81 Find a separate permanent storage place for odds and ends without a home that are hiding in your hall closet.

82 Return stray items from the hall closet to their designated storage place.

83 To improve the appearance of the closet, purchase matching hangers for coats and jackets.

84 Keep in your closet only the coats and jackets that are currently worn for the particular season.

85 Give each family member his own location in the closet for coats. If it's just two of you, visually divide the closet in half.

86 Arrange coats by seasons placing fall/winter jackets to the far sides of the closet and keeping spring/summer jackets front and center. Change the order around when the seasons change.

87 Place small wicker baskets or bins on the shelf above the clothing rod. Use these containers for winter gloves, hats and scarves and a basket for tote bags.

88 Store the vacuum cleaner in the closet only if there's no other convenient place for it.

89 Place a small rug on the closet floor. Upon arrival from home remove outdoor shoes and place them in the closet. The rug keeps dirt and small rocks from spreading all over the floor and is easily vacuumed.

Home Office—administrative central

Every home needs an office of some kind whether it's a built-in desk in the kitchen, a desk placed in the corner of the den or TV room, or a whole room. Organized systems keep the home office from becoming a cluttered muddle. Create a place for everything from paper clips to wrapping paper. The most important thing is to clear the desktop completely when you are finished working for the day. A desk is a work space not a storage area.

90 If you don't have a room to designate exclusively as an office, use a homemade or purchased desk with drawers to create an office in the family room, den or guest bedroom.

91 To make a large inexpensive desk, purchase a 6 or 8 foot x 2 foot laminate kitchen countertop from the hardware store. Lay it on top of two 2 drawer filing cabinets, one cabinet under each end of the countertop. With good lighting, a wall calendar, a phone, office supplies, computer and printer you have a designated place to conduct all home business transactions such as paying bills, doing computer work, and opening mail. If there's a TV nearby, better yet. You can do office work while watching TV.

92 For rock bottom prices, purchase office supplies when school supplies go on sale each summer and fall.

93 Designate only one drawer of your file cabinet or desk for everyday office supplies. This eliminates searching through multiple drawers for what you need. Always return items to the same place.

94 With a few of your everyday office supplies in one drawer of your desk or file cabinet, the whole family will know where they are. Be adamant about enforcing the rule of returning items to the drawer after use.

95 Keep the following in a desk drawer, with smaller items in a divided tray:

- paper clips
- binder clips in 2 sizes
- rubber bands
- stapler with a box of extra staples
- staple remover
- scotch tape
- scissors
- school eraser
- white-out

- book of stamps
- business cards
- 3 hole punch for 8 ½ x 11 paper
- Ruler or craftsman style measuring tape
- return address labels
- calculator
- washable glue
- rubber cement
- packing tape
- rubber stamps for decorating homemade cards
- 2 colored ink pads

96 Separate souvenir mugs on the counter can hold:

- washable felt markers
- permanent marker pens
- 3-4 pens
- 2-3 pencils

97 File folders in a filing cabinet are an efficient and organized way to store many items that otherwise become misplaced or are cumbersome to store. Label a folder in your desk's filing cabinet for *each* of the following:

- note pads for everyday use
- sheet protectors
- manila envelopes in small and large sizes
- address labels held together with a large binder clip

Take items out of the file folder when you need them and return to the folder afterwards.

98 Two other handy items for your office include:

- electric pencil sharpener—on the counter
- electric paper shredder—under the desk

99 Even though today's smartphones have built-in calculators, your phone may not be in your office when you need to crunch numbers. Purchase several small calculators for home and office use. Solar calculators last a long time and eliminate the need for purchasing and storing calculator batteries.

100 Pens seem to multiply like rabbits and then disappear, or the drawer is full of pens that don't work. Go through your stash when you're on the phone and toss the ones that don't write or are running out of ink. Same holds true for felt marker and permanent marker pens.

101 Keep only ½ dozen pens and pencils at a time, either in your desk drawer or in a favorite souvenir mug on the desk counter. Sharpen ½ dozen pencils all at once so they're ready to use when you need one.

102 Designate a separate drawer or bin for surplus office supplies that you purchased on sale: pencils, pens, scotch tape, post it notes, binder clips, rubber bands, note pads and permanent markers. You may want to make it your secret stash to keep family members from raiding it.

103 Purchase scotch tape and post it notes in bulk. Keep one of each, plus a pen, throughout the house—home office, kitchen, master bedroom, and children's bedroom and play room.

104 Save the rubber bands that come with the daily newspaper. Consistently wrap them onto a designated door knob to keep handy when needed.

105 Many nonprofit organizations send address labels in the mail. Send the organization a nominal donation. Use a large binder clip to keep labels together. Store the address labels in a file with mailing envelopes and manila envelopes.

106 Keep one book of stamps in your office and one in your purse or briefcase and you'll always have a stamp handy.

107 When computer paper goes on sale, consider purchasing a 10 ream box. The initial outlay will save you money in the long run since the paper will last a long time, perhaps even several years. Store the box of reams under your desk, out of sight but easily accessible.

108 The secret to a clutter-free office desk top is to have a home for every item. The 2nd secret is to return the item to its home after use.

109 If you find that your desk is still piled with odds n ends of stuff or paperwork, it's time to rethink your storage system: Does each item have a permanent storage location and you're just not putting it away? Or is the item's home incompatible with your organizational style and thus, doesn't get put away? Designate a new location or system and try again.

110 It may take several rounds of reorganizing your office supplies until you find a system that works for you. Keep at it, it's worth it.

111 Scissors are indispensable staples in every household. Purchase a half-dozen or more in different sizes and place in drawers in multiple rooms of the house including the kitchen, the playroom, home office and the master bathroom.

112 Purchase two full size scissors for cutting paper. Keep one pair in the home office for general use and another in a kitchen drawer for clipping coupons or cutting out magazine articles.

113 Purchase several pairs of blunt end paper scissors for the children's bedroom desk or the playroom.

114 Keep small scissors in the home office, the kitchen junk drawer and your bathroom. The next time you can't get that product wrapper off, the scissors will be handy. Immediately return the scissors to the designated drawer.

115 Keep two specialty kitchen shears in a kitchen drawer for cutting up food. Instruct family members how these shears differ from regular shears. Insist that they be used for food only.

116 Purchase the best quality sewing dressmaker shears that you can afford. Shears can be re-sharpened and will last for decades. Store the shears with your sewing supplies. Instruct family members that dressmaker shears are expensive and *only* used for cutting fabric. Other usage will ruin the blades and make the shears unsuitable for cutting cloth.

117 If you continue using a phone land line, keep a notebook by the main phone for writing down messages from the answering machine. Make it a rule in your home that if someone is not willing to take messages he/she is not allowed monitoring the answering machine.

118 If you like to write or journal and frequently put pen to paper with thoughts and ideas on anything and everything for using later, use spiral notebooks or decorative journals. Label the notebooks, if desired, for the subject matter.

119 Label one spiral notebook as a Wish Book for house and yard purchases you'd like to make. List the items on separate pages by cost:

- Under $100
- $100-$500
- $500-$1000

Refer to the list about every six months, adding or deleting items. By writing down your wishes they become instilled in your subconscious. Soon you'll be surprised at how many items you can cross off your list because they were on your mind and you purchased them without really thinking about it.

120 Order family cards on line at www.vistaprint.com or at an office supply store. Family cards are like business cards but with family information, as desired:

- Name
- Address
- Email
- Phone number, home and cell
- Fax, if you have one

121 Carry family cards in your wallet, briefcase and purse for handing to others. This saves you from digging for paper and pen to write this information for someone.

122 Place a work or family business card in your eyeglass case, offering a reward for returned glasses if lost.

Kitchen—the heart of the home

It seems as though everyone, whether family members or guests, enjoys gathering in the kitchen. You'll want your kitchen to reflect a tidy, uncluttered, welcoming atmosphere that will continue to draw folks.

123 Keep minimal items on the kitchen counter to maximize working space—one container for kitchen tools, a butcher block full of knives and perhaps a fruit bowl. Store the toaster, blender and stand mixer in a deep drawer or pantry shelf. If there's one appliance you use almost daily, keep it on the counter but hidden under a decorative cover.

124 Keep your most used kitchen tools—silicone spatulas, wooden spoons, cooking utensils—in a tall, open storage container on the counter near the stove. Tools are easy to see and reach. No more hunting through a drawer for the right tool.

125 Store your infrequently used, but needed, kitchen tools such as cooking tongs, turkey baster, wire whisk, potato masher or salad tongs in an open storage container in the cupboard. There when you need them, out of sight when you don't.

126 A kitchen drawer with multiple dividers separates like-sized small kitchen tools.

- One section can hold the smallest Tupperware seals such as sipper seals, tumbler/snack cup seals and midget seals.
- Another section holds metal tools such as can opener, vegetable peeler, pizza cutter, potato peeler, garlic press.
- Another section holds like-sized tools such as an egg separator, lettuce corer, mushroom brush and tea infuser.

When you open the drawer your small kitchen tools will be neat and organized and you can easily find the one you need.

127 Does your Tupperware fall out of your cupboards when you open the door? Or is your Tupperware everywhere and you can't find what you need when you need it? The first step to organizing it all is to sort it by size and locate the corresponding seal.

128 Only keep food storage containers that have matching seals. A container without a lid is useless for keeping food fresh in the refrigerator or freezer. If the lid is missing, move the container to the bathroom or craft room for organizing makeup, craft or sewing supplies.

129 The newest trend in kitchens is large deep drawers for storing dishes and other items that once were placed on kitchen shelves. One or two large drawers are a great place to keep your Tupperware. Organize containers by category— refrigerator, freezer and microwavable containers with seals or covers in one drawer.

130 A separate large storage drawer in the kitchen will hold Tupperware for storing snacks as well as containers needed for making school and work lunches like snack cups and sandwich keepers. This is also a place to store plastic plates and tumblers for every day use.

131 If you don't have the benefit of large storage drawers, with a little thought and planning, your kitchen shelves can adequately contain your Tupperware. For the ultimate in organization, designate certain shelves of the cupboards for your Tupperware so it's not strewn about in every cupboard of the kitchen.

132 For storing Tupperware snack cups and small storage bowls, use an uncovered, see-through plastic storage container. Select a size that fits the shelf and can be easily removed from the cupboard. A useful size is 16 x 12 inches/16 quarts. Stack the Tupperware containers inside the larger container. When looking for a specific piece of Tupperware or when unloading the dishwasher, just pull the container forward to remove, or place, Tupperware containers in it.

133 Use a separate 16 x 12 inch/16 quart see-through plastic storage container to keep the smaller cooking and baking items you use most often—2 sets of measuring cups plus 1 and 2 cup measuring pitchers, generic biscuit and cookie cutters. The container fits most cupboard shelves and can be easily pulled out or forward to access contents.

134 Seals, seals, seals—everywhere you look those plastic storage container seals are lurking. Handle the chaos once and for all with proper organization. Store the seals separately from the containers. Two open plastic baskets will fit side by side on most cupboard shelves. Use one approximately 11 inches wide x 13 inches deep for all round and square Tupperware seals 7 inches and smaller. File them in the basket by placing one in front of the other with the largest seals in the back. Pull the basket forward from the shelf and you'll quickly find the seal size you need.

135 For medium sized rectangular seals that go on Tupperware refrigerator and freezer containers, purchase a plastic basket approximately 8 inches wide and 11 inches deep. The basket will sit alongside the other basket of seals.

136 Store the corresponding rectangular and square refrigerator and freezer containers, nestled inside each other, on the shelf above the baskets of seals.

137 The largest freezer containers also need a home. Most times, these containers will be in the freezer filled with chicken, steaks, fish and other meat or food products purchased in bulk. When you have too many freezer containers in your cupboard it means it's time to go grocery shopping and replenish the freezer.

138 For short term storage of large freezer containers until they're replenished in the freezer with bulk food products, pull the baskets of Tupperware seals forward on the shelf and put the large freezer containers behind them. Store the matching seals under the containers. This is an out of the way place to store these larger containers yet maximizes your cupboard storage space. It would be awkward to store frequently used items behind the smaller baskets.

139 Since some food containers are microwave safe and others are not, it makes sense to store all microwaveable containers separately in one location. The most convenient storage area is a shelf or cupboard near the microwave. Store seals upright in a Tupperware seal holder next to the containers.

140 When you place containers of food in the freezer, label each with specially designed freezer labels. Write the contents and date on the label with a black permanent marker so you'll know which food items to use first.

141 If you have a freezer chart you can write the suggested "use by" date on the freezer label before adhering it to the food container.

142 Purchase two sets of measuring cups and measuring spoons. Invariably, you'll need a dry cup or spoon when one is wet or the size you need is in the dishwasher.

143 If you bake, create a cooking storage area for all the items you might use: mixing bowls of various sizes that nestle inside each other, a rolling pin, baking cake pans and other bake ware. This eliminates opening multiple drawers or cupboards to find what you need, saving you time and energy.

144 Holiday or seasonal cookie cutters can be stored in a tin bucket in your large baking drawer or placed in large zip-lock bags. Place them out of the way in a high cupboard until next Christmas when you use them most often.

145 Get rid of the small expensive tins of spices that are probably past their expiration date. Purchase spices from bulk bins at the discount store to save money.

146 Store spices in air-tight spice shakers on a carousel. Arrange spices alphabetically using labels to identify contents.

147 Store spices where you use them—in a cabinet next to the stove.

148 Every kitchen needs a junk drawer. It serves a two-fold purpose—as a mini-office for a notepad, a couple pens and pencils, rubber bands, small scissors, paper clips,

tape measure and ruler. The other use is as a catch-all for small misplaced items you found while vacuuming such as Legos.

149 Other useful items in a junk drawer could include small containers of various sized nails for hanging pictures, a small hammer, freezer labels for food items in the refrigerator or freezer along with a black permanent marker for writing date and contents.

150 If the kitchen is near the back door, store a spare pair of sunglasses for gardening, a hand pruner for cutting flowers and a craftsman measuring tape in your junk drawer.

151 It's bound to happen that the kitchen junk drawer eventually becomes a quick place to stash odds n ends of things that belong elsewhere. An older child or pre-teen will gladly re-organize it for you for a nominal fee. It can become a fun, traditional chore when "there's nothing to do."

152 Do you enjoy collecting seasonal dinnerware but lack kitchen storage space? Try this: wrap each piece in tissue paper and store in labeled bins in the garage. As each season arrives, display the dinnerware in a stacking plate holder on the kitchen counter or the dining room table. Set the table using these dishes. When the season is over, repack the dinnerware and return them to the garage. If this is too much trouble, perhaps it's time to donate some sets to a thrift store.

153 Replace your mismatched food serving pieces with neutral colored ones such as Corning ware French White. Neutral colors coordinate with all your dinnerware sets and eliminate the need for multiple serving sets.

154 The simplest way to reduce clutter in your kitchen is to stop purchasing more gadgets, widgets and other kitchen paraphernalia. The next time you're tempted to bring home a kitchen tool, ask yourself, "Is this a need or a want?" "How often will I use it?" "Do I already have a comparable item at home?" "Do I have a place to store it?" If you're honest with your answers, more times than not, you'll leave it at the store.

155 The kitchen is similar to the garage because there's usually more stuff in it than your family needs. Once a year, survey the contents of each cupboard. What haven't you used lately that you could donate or put in a garage sale? Which cupboard is the most challenging—the one where things don't fit properly and you find yourself muttering under your breath each time you need to get something out of it or put something into it? Tackle this cupboard first, marking an hour on your calendar to deal with it, then systematically move on to another distressing cupboard.

156 Keep a small step stool in the kitchen to reach items in the higher cabinets.

157 How many cookbooks does one household need? Preview your cookbook collection and determine which ones you actually use and which ones are just taking up space. Donate the cookbooks you rarely or never use to the library.

158 Make it a rule that if you buy a new cookbook, you must discard an existing one. This may make you think twice about purchasing another one.

159 When you receive or purchase a new cookbook, take the time to browse through or read it completely. Use a yellow highlighter to mark recipes you'd like to try. Use a sheet of loose leaf paper to write down the name of the recipe and page number for future use. Staple the sheet inside the cookbook for easy reference.

160 Organize your loose recipes by using:

- An index card box with labeled tabs—works best for recipes on 3x 5 cards. Review the recipes periodically and toss the ones you haven't used.

- A binder with pockets that hold 3x5 cards for your most frequently used recipes.
- A large 3 ring binder with sheet protectors and tabs for your personal custom cookbook. Sheet protectors keep your recipe dry and are easy to wipe clean if you spill.

161 As you clip recipes from magazines, either scotch tape or staple them to 3 x 5 cards or insert them into sheet protectors and file behind the corresponding tab in your custom cookbook binder according to these categories:

- Appetizers
- Main courses
- Salads
- Desserts
- Cookies
- Vegetables

162 Double the storage space under the kitchen sink by purchasing 2 tier wire cabinet organizers with slide out drawers from www.LTDCommodities.com. These space saving multi-level bins provide storage for kitchen cleaning supplies, scouring pads, dish and dishwasher soaps and more.

163 Dry goods comprise the basic food staples in your kitchen. They have a long shelf life yet come in plastic bags and boxes that are not air-tight and will cause contents to go stale. Boxes don't allow you to see the contents. Plastic bags don't stack. Once opened, the contents could spill making a mess in your cupboard. Since you want to keep your dry goods as fresh as possible for as long as you can, the quintessential containers for long term storage are air tight, see-through containers like Tupperware's modular products. You can buy them at a Tupperware party or on-line through your local representative.

164 When you purchase containers like Tupperware's modular containers, ask your sales representative to help you select the right size container—oval, rectangular or square—for every food item and staple in your cupboard or pantry. This maximizes your storage space and allows you to build a personalized comprehensive permanent storage system that will last you for years.

165 Using containers like Tupperware's modular products, organize your dry goods and staples into centers for easy access: baking center (flour, sugar, powdered sugar, brown sugar, baking soda, baking powder, salt); pasta/bean center; snack center (crackers, chips and cookies/granola bars, popcorn);

breakfast center (oatmeal, dry cereals, cream of wheat, granolas); beverage center (tea, coffee, hot chocolate, dry fruit drink mixes).

166 When you arrive home after grocery shopping immediately open the bags and boxes of dry goods and staples—cookies, crackers, chips, cereals, sugars, flour, rice, popcorn,—and empty contents into the matching labeled container. Make this activity a family habit. You'll find that school age children enjoy helping. Your pantry and cupboards stay well organized and all family members can quickly find the item they want. In addition, you'll save money since food stays fresh longer.

167 When repackaging food from boxes and plastic bags to permanent containers, don't throw out the cooking directions and/or recipes. Clip directions and recipes from the box or bag and file them in a recipe binder, staple to 3 x 5 cards and file in your recipe box or tape cooking directions to the outside of the container. Do not put the cooking directions or recipes inside the container with the food. Bugs are known to live in the glue of the box.

168 Keep the food container in its storage space on the shelf even when the contents are gone. A quick glance at the see-through windows when preparing your grocery list will tell you which items are low or gone and need to be replenished. Write down the item on your grocery shopping list.

169 Have you ever thought you were out of canned tomatoes only to find several cans later in a different cupboard? Store your canned goods in one location whether on shelves in the pantry or a selected cabinet.

170 Arrange canned goods in rows by category—fruits, vegetables, spaghetti and other jars of sauces, canned meats such as chili, chicken or tuna, canned tomato products, canned soups, cake and brownie mixes, canned frostings, canned beans. Group items in glass bottles together—syrup, vegetable and olive oils, vinegars.

171 Rotate your grocery stock. Place recently purchased canned goods in the back and move the current ones to the front, just like they do at the store. Even canned goods have a shelf life with an expiration date on each can.

172 With your canned goods all in one location and organized by category, it's easy to put groceries away and helps you see what items to purchase on your next shopping trip. In addition family members can find the needed item quickly.

173 As soon as groceries have been put away, place the reusable grocery bags near the front or back door to take to the car the next time you go out.

174 Create zones in your refrigerator to easily see what's there. Designate specific locations for eggs, dairy products, deli meats, fresh meat, fruits and vegetables.

175 Set aside an area in your refrigerator for leftover meals. Store leftovers in microwavable Tupperware containers. These products go from the refrigerator to the freezer to the microwave to the table. A quick glance in the refrigerator lets family members know what there is to eat for a snack or a meal or take to work for lunch.

176 Clean out the refrigerator weekly before grocery shopping, tossing forgotten leftovers.

177 If some family members require special foods, give each a section of the refrigerator so they can easily find their food.

178 Refrigerate opened canned food in air tight containers like Tupperware. Square or rectangular containers are more space-efficient than round ones.

179 Use containers like Tupperware to make entrees, salads and appetizers ahead of time for family meals, parties and other get-togethers. At meal time simply remove the seal and place the container on the table or transfer the food to a microwavable container to reheat.

180 Designate a vegetable bin in the refrigerator for children's snacks. Fill it with cheese sticks, juice boxes, yogurt, cut up vegetables and other healthy treats. Children can easily help themselves to after school snacks.

181 Keep an air-tight container on a shelf in the cupboard or pantry where children can access it. Fill the container with healthy snacks such as granola bars, individual packs of whole wheat crackers or cookies, fruit roll-ups and the like. These are "parent-approved" snacks and reduce the probability of kids eating too many high calorie-laden treats.

182 If you use food coloring that comes in small not-so-liquid—tight bottles, consider putting them in a sealed container with a paper towel on the bottom of the container. If the bottles leak, the spill stays in the container with the paper towel absorbing it. Your cupboard or pantry stays clean.

183 Most of us have large food storage containers, gallon pitchers, serving trays, cake platters, large bowls and other serving pieces that we use occasionally for family get-togethers and parties. The problem is where to store them when not in use. Purchase a see-through plastic storage container with a latching lid like your other containers but big enough for your additional serving pieces. If there's sufficient space in a pantry, utility room or basement, keep the container there. Otherwise, store the container in the garage or shed.

184 No matter how bad the party mess looks at night, if left disorderly, it will look worse in the morning. If you and your partner clean it up together at night after your guests leave, it's a great time to talk about how the party went and who said what to whom.

185 Keep a tempered glass, heat resistant board on the kitchen countertop. It's handy for placing items removed from the microwave or oven or for quick cutting jobs without hauling out another cutting board. It's easy to clean when countertops are wiped down.

186 When preparing food in the kitchen, pull the wastebasket out from under the sink and keep near your work area. This makes it easier to dispose of garbage and aids with clean up.

Linen Closet—functional and tidy

Keep your linen closet functional and organized so you'll be pleased at what you see every time you open it. In addition you'll easily find what you're looking for. Use it for its purpose—storing towels, bed linens, blankets and comforters and other bedroom and bath objects, not as a catch-all for other non-related items.

187 Purchase towel sets in two colors only—one color for guests, another color for family use. Guest towels stay new looking longer since they are used less frequently.

188 Each family member only needs a minimum of towels—two bath towels, two or three hand towels, two or three washcloths. Otherwise, keep only as many towels as will neatly fit in your linen closet. Designate a shelf for bath towels and another shelf for hand towels and washcloths.

189 Purchase two sheet sets for each bed in the house. When one set is removed for laundering, you can immediately make the bed with the other set.

190 Buy two decorator sheet sets and designate them for the guest bedroom. When guests depart, immediately remove the sheets and replace with fresh linens. The guest room is now ready for your next overnight visitors whenever that may be.

191 With sheet sets designated specifically for the guest bedroom, you won't need to sort through your whole linen collection searching for acceptable looking sheets for the guest bed.

192 If you only have one set of good sheets for the guest bedroom, when guests depart, wash and dry the set then make the bed. Guest bed will be ready for the next guests.

193 Use containers with lids to house extra bar soap, family size bottles of body wash, lotion and other toiletries. Label bins. Store these containers in the linen closet. Contents are out of sight, neatly organized and there as you need them.

Living Room/Family Room—the family's social center

In some homes the living room is only used for reading or conversing with family and friends. In other homes, it's the primary social room of the house. The challenge is to keep it presentable while functioning as a family-friendly room for multiple activities.

194 To keep dirt from being tracked inside, make it a family routine to remove shoes upon entering the house. Keep a large basket by the front door for shoes.

195 If some family members wear different styles of shoes in a week's time, encourage them to hand carry shoes to their bedroom closet upon entering the house eliminating an accumulation of shoes by the front door.

196 Have each family member designate one pair of shoes to be worn inside the house—sneakers, slip-ons, non-skid slippers or shoes, sandals—shoes that won't mar the floor.

197 If you have wood or laminate floors in the main rooms of your house, ban stocking feet. It's too easy for both the young and the old to slip and fall. In addition, shoes provide foot support on hard floors.

198 Since the living room doubles as a playroom in some homes, store a few toddler toys in a bin tucked behind an end table or large chair. A separate bin for books keeps them handy for story time while cuddling on the sofa with family members.

199 If your living room doubles as your TV room, put the TV in an armoire or large unit with doors that close. It's there when you want to watch TV and out of sight when entertaining. The lower shelves of the unit can hide the DVD, CD players and cable units.

200 Tuck a small kid-size table with 2 chairs against a living room wall for little ones to do crafts or color. Toys can be stored underneath.

201 Keep tabletop decorative items to a minimum to reduce time spent moving them when dusting. In addition, fewer knickknacks make the room appear less cluttered.

202 Use a microfiber dusting mitt since it picks up the dust rather than moving it around.

203 Keep only the most current magazines on a coffee table. When finished reading them, transfer them to the recycle bin.

204 A trunk doubles as a coffee table and a place to store floor pillows and cozy quilts.

205 Many of us enjoy burning candles in our homes but aren't mindful of keeping our supplies stocked. Be mindful of checking your supply as the fall season begins and purchase tapers, votive candles and tea lights. Store each variety in a labeled container.

206 If you purchase all candles in one scent such as vanilla, you can mix candle styles-tapers, jars, votives and tea lights—throughout your living areas without conflicting aromas.

207 Refillable scented oil warmers such as Glade and electric wickless candles like Scentsy provide an orderly, cleaner and safer alternative to candles yet provide long lasting scent. Keep refills in a bin in the linen closet or master bathroom.

208 Do you oftentimes miss the start of your favorite show because you can't find the remote? Designate a small, cloth lined wicker basket or small tray to hold the TV and DVD controls. Keep the basket in full view on the ottoman or coffee table. You'll no longer need to dig under the sofa cushions for lost controls.

Master Bathroom—privacy please

The master bathroom could without a doubt be the most disorderly room in the house. Why? It's a private place. It's located away from the other rooms. Other family members rarely go in there and guests certainly don't see it. You're in it getting ready in the morning and then may not venture back into it until later in the day or evening. It's easy to let it go and have it be a dumping ground for toiletries, make-up and grooming aids that don't get put away. Make this room one to be proud of by decorating it fashionably, organizing its many contents and putting things in their proper place after using them.

209 Use sectioned trays or small individual open containers in your bathroom drawers. Each section can store separate categories of related items:

- daily makeup such as moisturizer, concealer, foundation, face powder, blush, eye shadows, mascara, eye lash curler
- makeup brushes
- hairbrush and comb, deodorant, toothpaste, toothbrush and dental floss
- nail file, nail clippers, eyebrow tweezers

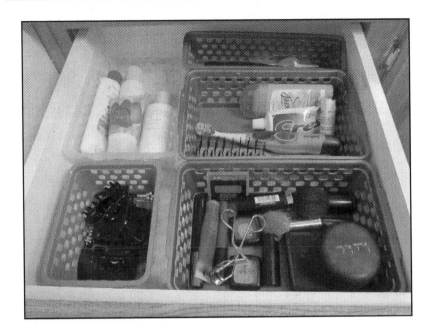

210 Designate a separate bathroom drawer for less frequently used items. All items should be neatly organized in small bins or divided trays:

- nail polish and remover
- purse size hand sanitizers
- spare hairbrushes and combs
- other infrequently used face and eye makeup
- sunscreen
- spare dental floss
- small tubes of toothpaste
- Band-Aids

211 Since most bathrooms rarely have enough storage space, you can double the storage capacity by using two tier wire organizers. The cabinet under the sink usually does not have shelves. The two tier organizers solve that problem. They have 2 shelves and fit the length of the cabinet. Use the top shelf of the organizer to keep every day toiletries handy yet off the counter such as body lotion, baby powder, hair spray, hair mousse. Use the lower slide out drawer for medications, vitamins and other pharmacy items but only if there are no young children in your home. If you have a long cabinet with 2 sinks, you can put an organizer under each sink.

212 What do you do with numerous decorative collectibles that you want to keep but have run out of places to display them? They can be pretty and functional in the bathroom. Use a tiny bud vase for small makeup brushes. A fancy mirrored tray can hold moisturizers and face creams. What about that pretty ceramic canister? Store cotton balls and Q-tips in it.

213 The bathroom countertop is as difficult to keep clutter free as your office desktop. Limit the number of permanent objects to display—decorative canisters with useful items, a plant or candle. Then make a permanent home for any other items you're tempted to keep on the countertop.

214 Each day make it a goal to restore the master bathroom to its pristine condition before you leave the room. Put everything away in its place after usage—makeup and hair brushes in the drawer, hair dryer in another drawer and hairspray on a shelf under the sink. It only takes about 15-20 seconds to do so. You'll be rewarded with a continually tidy bathroom.

215 Designate bathroom drawers, shelves and bins for him and her. Grooming needs are different. Each person can find what he/she needs and each is only responsible for keeping his/her personal items organized.

216 Use two clothes hampers—a large one for clothes washed on the regular washing machine cycle, a smaller hamper for clothing you'll wash on the delicate cycle.

217 Keep a plastic basket of cleaning supplies under the sink in every bathroom. With cleaning supplies in each bathroom, it's convenient to do a quick clean of the sinks, mirrors, toilets and countertops without having to drag supplies in from another room.

218 Limit your cleaning supplies to four basics: a glass cleaner, an all—purpose cleaner, a disinfectant and a tub/tile cleaner.

219 Keep old washcloths in the linen closet for use as cleaning cloths. Hang them on the edge of the clothes hamper to dry then wash with the regular laundry.

220 Purchase "green" cleaning products that are non-caustic, promote cleaner indoor air quality and will not cause irreversible harm to children if accidentally swallowed.

221 Stock up on small sizes of shower gel, hand lotion, bubble bath and anti-bacterial gel at the twice yearly Bath and Body Works sale. Store them in a labeled bin under the bathroom sink or in the linen closet.

222 Small size toiletries that are 3 ounces or less make perfect supplies for your carry—on bag when flying. They also make great gifts for house guests or any time a gift is needed unexpectedly.

223 From www.thebudgetfashionista.com According to a March 9, 2000, FDA report (revised October 15, 2002), "Consumers should be aware that expiration dates are simply 'rules of thumb,' and that a product's safety may expire long before the expiration date if the product has not been properly stored." Here is a guideline to help determine when it's time to toss out old makeup:

- Foundation: 3-6 months
- Concealer: Wand applicator concealers should be tossed within 6 months since they're likely to grow bacteria. Stick, twist-up tubes, or compact concealers can last up to 12 months, especially if you use a <u>makeup brush</u> to apply the product.
- Pressed powder cosmetics: Facial powder, <u>blush</u> and eye shadow should be thrown out after one year. If you get an eye infection, however, you'll have to toss out any eye shadow you've used, to avoid re-infecting yourself.
- Lip gloss and lipstick: 1 year
- Mascara: You should always replace mascara after 3 months. Toss it immediately if it becomes dry, or you develop an eye infection. Remember: never, ever share mascara.
- Eye and lip pencils: If you sharpen them every few days, makeup pencils can last a year or longer. It's time to trash them when they become dry, crumbly, or hard to apply.
- All-natural cosmetics: Because these products do not contain preservatives, they should be used or discarded within 6 months.

Master Bedroom—cozy and comfortable

Your Master Bedroom should be a tidy, organized, serene place to read, relax and sleep. Make it your goal to keep it as neat as the ones in the home magazines and don't allow it to become a catch-all room.

224 Keep bed dressings simple. Insert a comforter into a duvet cover with an all season motif. Just fluff the pillows, straighten the sheets, pull up the duvet cover and arrange the decorative pillows if you use them. *Viola!* The bed is made. Have similar coverings for your kids' beds.

225 Make the bed in the morning as soon as the last person is out of it. If you delay any longer, chances are it won't get made.

226 Ask your spouse to help you make the bed on weekends. It gives you one more opportunity to talk and be together for a few minutes. In addition, making the bed takes even less time with four hands.

227 Designate nightstands as a clutter free zone. Keep them eye-appealing. Limit items on the nightstand to a small vase of fresh flowers, a favorite decorative item or family picture and a reading lamp. Place a 23W compact fluorescent bulb (100 watt incandescent equivalent) in the lamp for good lighting. If you enjoy reading in bed, keep just a book or two on your nightstand along with a spare pair of reading glasses.

228 If you enjoy reading inspirational materials each day, place your book or electronic tablet on your nightstand before retiring each evening. Set your clock for a few minutes earlier so you have some time to read before you arise. This gets the day off to a good start and saves you the time of looking around for where you left your book.

229 Keep a small, decorative dish on top of your dresser for the items you wear everyday—watch and rings. The items will be easy to find and put on each day.

230 If you don't have a large jewelry box, separate necklaces and bracelets in muffin tins, ice cube trays or small plastic bowls. Place the containers in a bureau drawer to keep out of sight.

231 Wrap the inside and outside of several shoe boxes with decorator contact paper. Fill one dresser drawer with boxes, side by side. Use for:

- Dark trouser socks
- Dark crew socks
- Sport socks and white socks

232 Use shoe boxes in other drawers to organize:

- pantyhose and tights
- Scarves
- Belts

233 Keep only clothes that are ready to wear in your closet. That means missing buttons re-attached, clothes pressed, torn hems repaired. When your business clothes are clean, pressed and hanging in your closet in wearable condition, you can lie in bed a few extra minutes in the morning thinking about your clothing choices, rather than fretting about "is a button missing?" "Does it need to be ironed?" "Did I repair that hem?"

234 If you think you'll never get around to sewing on the missing button or hemming those pants, pay a seamstress to do it or put it in a bag for the thrift store. Why fill your closet with clothing that isn't presentable to wear?

235 If you're trying to decide whether to keep a clothing item, ask yourself, "When was the last time I wore it?" The answer tells you whether you like it or not.

236 Arrange clothing in your closet by category:

- Jackets
- Pants

- Blouses/ shirts
- Sweater sets
- Skirts
- Dresses
- Suits

237 Hang blouses, T-shirts and shirts by color. It's easier to find the right top when they're grouped together.

238 If your closets are spacious enough, arrange clothing in your closet according to the seasons. If space is a concern, pack your exclusively winter or summer clothes in storage bins or dust free clothing bags and transfer to another closet until next season.

239 The end of each season is a good time to discard the clothes you didn't wear.

240 Keep a large paper grocery bag in your closet so when you decide you no longer want that blouse, pair of pants, purse, or whatever, you can place it in the bag. When the bag is full, take it to the front door to take to the car and drop it off at a donation center or thrift store the next time you do errands.

241 Ask the thrift store receptionist for a tax deductible receipt. Fill out the receipt while the items you donated are still fresh in your mind. Put the receipt in your wallet. During your routine wallet cleaning, place the receipt in the tax deductible folder.

242 Keep closets neat and tidy by using the same style and same size hangers for everyone's clothes. Hangers become inter-changeable among family members, as needed.

243 Don't kick your shoes off onto the floor of the closet. Some folks keep the boxes the shoes came in, label each and return shoes to the box after usage, neatly stacking the boxes in the closet. Others have a floor rack that holds several dozen pairs of shoes. A shoe organizer that hangs from the clothing rod and holds six or more pairs of shoes, keeps shoes near eye level and makes for a neat closet appearance. The important thing is to find a shoe organizer that works well in your closet yet make sure it's one you'll utilize.

244 What to do with all those shoes? Transfer summer shoes and sandals to an under-the-bed storage container for the winter. This is a good time to donate the shoes you didn't wear this summer to the thrift store. At the end of winter, retrieve your summer shoes and put the winter shoes away in that same storage container under the bed.

245 Only keep three pairs of tennis shoes:

- The ones you just bought
- The ones replaced by the new pair
- Your oldest pair for washing the car and working in the garden

Each time you purchase a new pair of tennis shoes, discard the oldest pair.

Outdoor Shed—extra space for your stuff

An outdoor shed is a useful building for housing items commonly stored in the garage. In addition, a shed frees up garage space for the family's vehicles.

246 Store these items in the shed during the winter months if you live in a climate where snow and ice eliminate the use of them:

- Bicycles
- Motorcycle
- Lawn chairs
- Outdoor patio furniture
- Picnic cooler
- Beach and patio umbrellas
- Lawn tractor
- Gardening cart
- Garden hoses
- Large garden tools
- Gardening soils and compost in storage bins with lids
- Flower pots

247 Another possibility is to consider limiting the outdoor shed to equipment needed for one activity such as gardening, outdoor sports or seasonal storage containers.

248 If your house doesn't have an office, a spare room or a basement, an outdoor shed can work well for your home-based business. Set up a desk for administrative paperwork. Install shelving to house your products. Hang a clock on the wall. Add an indoor heater during cold months to keep warm.

249 If your shed is large enough, hang shelves or purchase ready-made shelves or steel wall units to store your belongings.

250 Remember that the shed is a storage place similar to the garage but on a smaller scale. It needs to be cleaned out periodically to keep clutter to a minimum.

Storage—there is a place for everything

If you look carefully around your house, you'll find smart, useable storage areas in nearly every room. For additional storage space, look *up* and look *inside*.

251 Shelves can hang in every room—on walls, above doorways and windows. They can be installed inside spare room closets, above the existing shelf in closets and inside utility and kitchen cabinets. Shelves come in various lengths and depths, decorative or plain, crafted of different wood types and can be painted to match your décor.

252 Use shelves to hold anything that would otherwise take up counter space in the kitchen, on tables or on your desk such as:

- Books
- Decorator items
- Framed photos
- Collectibles
- Laundry supplies including laundry baskets
- Craft and hobby supplies
- Cleaning supplies
- Toiletries
- Children's toys
- Small kitchen appliances

253 Shoebox size plastic containers with latched lids are ideal storage containers. Unlike cardboard boxes, they won't deteriorate over time. Latched lids keep contents from falling out if tipped. Clear ones are best for viewing the contents inside.

Containers stack easily on shelves and on top of each other. They can be purchased for a few dollars at retail and craft stores. Use for:

- Miscellaneous sewing supplies—bias tapes, elastic, Velcro, lace and more.
- Rubber crafting stamps and ink pads
- Scrapbooking supplies
- Curling ribbon, bows and other fabric ribbons for wrapping packages
- Birthday decorating supplies
- House tool kit
- Shoe polishes and rags
- Small bottles of hotel hand and body lotions, conditioners and shampoos
- Gift supply of small bottles of lotions, bath gels and body wash
- Tea lights, votive and other candles

254 Purchase paper towels and toilet paper in bulk to save money. Where to store it all? Put 2-3 rolls of paper towels under each sink in every bathroom, under the kitchen sink and in the laundry room. Stack ½ dozen rolls of toilet paper in the cabinet of every bathroom.

255 Put a large, round table-to-floor cloth over a round table to create hidden storage area underneath. Stack shoebox size containers underneath.

256 Use magnetic acrylic photo frames to display pictures on the refrigerator, file cabinet or any magnetic surface. These reduce the number of standing photo frames throughout your house. Frames come in various sizes and are available at most craft stores.

257 What to do with gift wrap paper, ribbon, bows, and gift tags? Store in an under bed storage container. Add a roll or two of scotch tape and 2 pairs of small scissors. Your gift wrapping supplies are all in one place yet out of sight when not needed.

258 To save on wrapping paper, purchase rolls of all occasion wrap for all gift occasions.

259 To save even more on wrapping paper, purchase rolls of white butcher paper as gift wrap. Have your little aspiring artists draw on the paper or use the paper plain tied with brightly colored yarn.

260 Use small wicker baskets or plastic bins to store winter gear. Use one for gloves, one for knitted hats and another one for scarves. Place bins with winter accessories on shelves in the utility or mud room or in upper shelves of the hall closet.

261 During the wintry cold months, keep the glove basket near the door used most often when entering and exiting the house. As family members come in, have them drop their gloves/mittens in the basket instead of stuffing them in coat pockets. If anyone wears a different coat on the next outing, gloves are readily available without having to remember which coat pockets they're in.

262 Keep multi-purpose cloth tote bags of various sizes in a closed cabinet or a bin in the hall closet. Use tote bags for:

- Books, magazines, DVDs, and CD's for car road trips
- Children's toys, books or games on the plane
- Your latest craft project
- Lunch tote
- For letter and bills to mail while running errands

263 Purchase a large covered storage bin for each child when they start grade school. Label each bin with child's name. Limit what you'll save as school days' memorabilia to just one bin per child. As each finishes school and the bin is full, give it to them for a graduation gift.

Utility Room/Mud Room—a multi-purpose bonanza

Whether large or small, this room is a bonus to any home. It offers a place to do laundry, has space for storage and serves as a back entrance in and out of the home where coats, jackets, umbrellas and shoes can be deposited.

264 Make washing clothes a family activity. Teach your spouse and older children how to sort clothes and use the washing machine and dryer. Demonstrate the quantity of detergent, bleach and fabric softener to use and where these products go in the machines. Assign older children to load the wash, dry and fold clothes. Rotate the duty among family members. When your children go away to college they'll be grateful for this knowledge and expertise.

265 When clean, washed and dried clothes have been folded and sorted for each family member, each person over the age of five is responsible for collecting their clothes and putting them away where they belong.

266 Instill a non-negotiable, unwritten rule in your household that if someone takes clothes out of the clothes dryer they are obligated to neatly layer each item in a pile, or preferably, fold each item. Dry underwear and socks may be tossed into a laundry basket. Otherwise, stuffing clean clothes into a laundry basket and making a wrinkled mess of everything is not allowed.

267 Take the basket of clean underwear and socks to the TV room to fold as you watch a favorite show.

268 Purchase laundry detergent, bleach and dryer towels before you run out. If you have room for storage, buy in bulk.

269 Store 2-3 laundry baskets, nestled inside each other, on a high out of the way shelf in the utility room when not in use.

270 Place a large, inexpensive indoor/outdoor carpet on the floor of your utility/mud room. This keeps the floor dry from wet shoes. Dirt is contained in the rug and can easily be vacuumed.

271 Encourage family members to remove shoes upon entering the house. Keep a large basket for shoes near the door.

272 The cabinets in your utility room are a good place to keep many household items:

- spare light bulbs
- extension cords and timers in a bin
- batteries in a container
- candles in containers
- flower vases
- frequently used baseball caps
- gloves in a bin
- dog leash and toys
- reusable water bottles
- shoe polish with polishing cloths
- furniture polish with dusting mitt
- spare flashlights
- bulk cleaning supplies
- umbrellas

273 A coat rack keeps frequently worn jackets handy. Hang jackets and coats according to the season. In the spring, hang light jackets or sweaters. In the winter move the lighter jackets and replace with heavy winter coats or fleece jackets.

274 Store a wastebasket under the sink in the utility room.

275 If your utility sink is in a cabinet, double the storage space under the sink by purchasing 2 tier wire cabinet organizers with slide out shelves from www.LTDCommodities.com. These space saving, multi-level bins provide storage for numerous items such as:

- Cleaning supplies
- Dog lease, brush and toys
- Shoe polishes and shoe brushes
- Dusting mitt and furniture wax or polish
- Rags for household use

PART TWO
Organize your Life

Christmas—the most wonderful time of the year

Christmas should be a joyful and happy time for celebrating the reason for the season with family and friends. An early start to Christmas preparations, pre-planning and organization go a long way towards making Christmas a peaceful holiday with little, if any, stress.

276 Some years Thanksgiving is the last week of November. That seems to make Christmas come earlier. Plan accordingly. Put the decorations up the weekend after Thanksgiving. You'll have one major task completed and can enjoy the decorations longer.

277 Just after Thanksgiving, set a date for completion of all Christmas tasks. Mark a day on the calendar by when everything needs to be done. This is your "due date." This is the single best gift and best stress-buster you can give yourself. A good date to choose is the last day of school before Christmas vacation or the day before your college kids arrive home. By that date, presents must be purchased and wrapped; the baking completely done and stored in Tupperware. The tree is up and decorated; the house is decorated; thorough dusting and house vacuuming competed. The laundry hampers are empty. Christmas dinner planned and non-perishables purchased. Then it's time to let the merry-making begin as you can relax and enjoy your family.

278 Get out your calendar and mark dates of all pre-Christmas commitments—the office party, the club get-together, your friend's annual party, the school Christmas pageant. Verify the dates of school vacation and college break.

279 Schedule a day to shop for the Christmas tree as a family.

280 Schedule the days you'll bake.

281 Make your last pre-Christmas shopping trip to the grocery store no less than five days before Christmas. After that the stores are extremely crowded and many Christmas grocery items are depleted.

282 Know your Christmas party limit and that of your family. If you think you or your family is over-scheduled, politely decline the non-essential get-togethers.

283 If you don't enjoy doing something, don't do it. It shouldn't matter to you if your neighbor has a lighted tree in every room and luminaries gracing the walkways. If that's just too much for you, decorate at a level that suits your time and energy.

284 Did your best friend hold 2 Christmas parties, a birthday party for 16, sewed a Christmas quilt and organized a Toy Drive as a community service project? If it's not your cup of tea, don't do it. You only need to please yourself. Explain to your family what your personal limits are and ask them to abide.

285 Compose your family Christmas letter the first week after Thanksgiving. Limit your letter to one page. Save it on the computer to print later.

286 When a Christmas card arrives in the mail, open it and place it at one of the place settings of the family dinner table. Have a family member read it out loud at dinner so all can share in the receiving of the card. Place the card in the designated holder until after the holidays.

287 Use a holiday basket, bread basket or large platter as the designated place for Christmas cards received.

288 After the holidays, put the photos and photo cards in your photo box or toss them.

289 Christmas cards make pretty and practical bookmarks.

- Use a paper cutter to cut the cards into 1 ½ inch wide strips, keeping different portions of the design intact. Punch a hole in the top of each bookmark and pull yarn through to make a tassel.
- Use binder clips to keep 8-10 bookmarks together. Place the bookmarks wherever you keep books—in or near an office desk, a coffee table in the living room, a book case, or in your nightstand drawer.
- Distribute bookmarker sets to your family and friends at your next get-together. If you work in an office, put the bookmakers on the office magazine/book exchange table for your co-workers.

290 Do your Christmas gift shopping in November or early December. The best selections of everything are in shorter supply the longer you wait.

291 Purchase large, clear storage bins with latching lids for your Christmas decorations. Cardboard boxes will eventually deteriorate. Plastic bins keep out the mice and insects if your decorations are stored in the garage or an outdoor shed.

292 Keep all receipts for items purchased as gifts. Write the gift recipient's name on it. Place receipts in an envelope in your bill box until after Christmas when you're sure there are no gifts to return or exchange. Then toss or shred the receipts.

293 Life is too short to get stressed out over a gift you purchased that the recipient doesn't want or like. Let them off the hook. Inform every family member that all gifts are returnable, you have the receipts and your feelings won't be hurt. It truly is the thought that counts.

294 Keep a few extra gifts on hand for unexpected needs. Kitchen towels, holiday hand towels, jar candles and note cards are always welcome.

295 The dinner hour and evenings are the best time to shop, especially on week nights. There are very few customers around and you'll be able to get the clerk's attention.

296 Avoid weekend shopping if at all possible. If you do shop on the weekend, go early Saturday or Sunday morning and plan to be home by noon.

297 Purchase replacement bulbs for the tree as soon as they arrive in the store early in November. These run out quickly and usually are not re-ordered.

298 Kick off the holiday season by planning a pre-Christmas outing with your spouse or a loved one early in December. Purchase tickets for a Christmas play or concert and go out for dinner. Get all dressed up to make it an event out of the ordinary.

299 Purchase a container specifically designed for holding gift wrap. It's tall for keeping rolls of wrapping paper upright and has a lid. After Christmas, store it in the garage or shed with the other Christmas decorations. Wrapping paper will be out of the way and stay dry in its container.

300 Christmas lists allow you to manage your budget by picking and choosing from among the desired presents.

301 Ask for Christmas lists from each family member. State that you'd like the lists before Thanksgiving. Who will deny a parent who writes: "I want to spend money on you. Do you want me to buy what I want you to have or what you want? Please send Christmas list." You'll be amused when your college son's list shows up via text message or email 2 days later, 3 pages long with websites and pictures.

302 Make shopping a date night. Schedule an early weeknight dinner at your favorite restaurant with your spouse. Go over the Christmas gift list together and then go shopping.

303 Christmas shopping can be done throughout the year. You know your family well enough to purchase some of what they'd like for Christmas. You'll have more time to shop sales, peruse the stores and not be rushed.

304 For gifts purchased throughout the year, select a large storage container with a latching lid. Store the gifts in the container in the garage. As Christmas approaches, just add an additional gift or two from their list and you're done.

305 When your budget is tight for family gift giving, ask your child what would disappoint him the most to not find under the tree on Christmas morning. This helps your child set realistic expectations and helps you know which gift to concentrate on.

306 Children aged four to seven may have no idea what they'd like for Christmas. If this is the case, take them to the toy store without them knowing your agenda and walk through the aisles. Take time to see what they linger over and ask why they like it, or discuss why it's not a good value. Make mental notes and you can put together a list on their behalf.

307 Before you go Christmas shopping, write down what you intend to purchase for each family member for

Christmas including stocking stuffers. Carry the notebook with you. Check each item off your list when purchased. This keeps you focused, within your budget and limits impulse buying.

308 If you'll be home for the holidays, set aside a full day about one week before Christmas to wrap presents. Enlist your spouse and make it a private party. Put on Christmas music, thaw a few cookies and talk about why you purchased what for whom. This is also a good time for your spouse to see what you two are giving this year instead of him being as surprised on Christmas Day as the recipient.

309 Planning to be away from home for Christmas? Decorate your house just enough to show some Christmas spirit. Those 2 or 3 storage bins that you'll need should be labeled properly so you can locate them and not have to dig through all your bins of decorations.

310 Learn from your own experience each year. If you delayed decorating the gingerbread house until Dec 24 so out of town family members could help and it was a timing disaster, you'll know not to do that again.

311 Create a master Christmas card list on the computer using the current year's cards that you received. Add each family's name, address, city, state and zip code. Next year you could use mail merge to create mailing labels even though hand addressed envelopes are more personal.

312 If you don't know where to begin in creating a master Christmas card list, try this: After you've addressed all your cards this year but before mailing them, carry them to the computer and create a master card list using the mailing information on each envelope. It takes about five minutes to do this and the following year you won't have to search everywhere for addresses.

313 Set aside a couple weeknight evenings for you and your spouse to do Christmas cards. It's more fun to do it together, talking and sharing as you go.

314 After Christmas, sort through the cards you received, adding folks to your master list that sent you a card if you want to reciprocate next year.

315 If you notice that a family has a new return address on the card they sent you, keep the envelope with all your other cards so you can make a notation of the new address on your master card list after Christmas.

316 Store holiday CD's and children's holiday books in a container with the rest of your Christmas decorations.

317 Get the baking done *early* in December. Sugar cookies can be baked ahead and frozen, unfrosted, in containers like Tupperware for several weeks.

318 If it's less stressful for you to make the cookie dough and bake them on your own without help from the kids and/or you can get it done faster, that's fine. Do whatever it takes.

319 Thaw and frost sugar cookies as you need them, then store in air-tight containers for a week.

320 Bake only the 2 or 3 goodies your family loves best instead of slaving away at a dozen varieties they eat only because they're there.

321 If sugar cookies are your family's favorite goodie, bake a double batch of at least 12 dozen, the first week of December. Thaw and frost them closer to Christmas.

322 Bake a second batch of your family's favorite cookies just to give away to friends and neighbors or to have on hand when unexpected guests drop in.

323 Create at least one family tradition that involves baking. Enlist the whole family when frosting the cookies. Take pictures. As the years move on, you'll have memorable photos of the kids when they were young, or the time they frosted cookies with a fiancée, or the first time they came home for Christmas as a married couple. Then there's the first time the grandkids frosted the traditional Christmas cookie—you got the pictures.

324 The first weeks of December are the time to make double dinner recipes and freeze half. You can easily pull these out for quick meals any night of the week.

325 Check your inventory of toilet paper, paper towels and napkins. Stock up early in December.

326 Is your camera ready for Christmas? Make sure its memory card is empty. Does the camera have fresh batteries or is it fully charged? Do camera prep at least a week before Christmas so the camera is ready to go. If your camera uses batteries, keep ½ dozen nearby so you don't have to go looking for them when you need them.

327 Remember to take time for you. Schedule time for a massage, manicure or pedicure, not as a chore, but as a relaxing break.

328 Make a Plan B in case Plan A falls apart. Be flexible and go with it.

329 Plan ahead for next year. When the holidays are over, pull out a notebook and evaluate. What worked this year? What didn't? What would you like to do differently next year?

330 Make a list of items needed for next year: replacement Christmas bulbs inside and outside the house, extension cords and timers for outdoor lights. Replenish Christmas card stock while cards are on sale. Catch the after Christmas sales for wrapping paper, bows, ribbons and gift tags.

Dealing with Paper—less is better

Rather than reduce paper it seems as though the electronic age generates more paper than ever. The challenge is to control it and not allow it to control you.

331 Limit the papers you bring into the house. Just because someone handed it to you at a meeting or event, doesn't mean you have to accept or keep it. If you take the handout but you don't want to keep it, recycle it before going home.

332 An In basket is nothing more than a temporary holding place for whatever paper items it contains. The items must be removed, sorted and placed in a permanent designated folder or file. Otherwise, an In basket is just another word for clutter.

333 If papers continue to collect on your office desk, it's possible that each paper's storage location isn't suitable enough. Rethink a location so it's handy and convenient for you to put it in its place.

334 Clear your home desk to its bare bones before you end your work for the day.

335 Create an indoor mailbox in a convenient location where it's handy but not in the way. A four-sided tray or basket works best. Whoever brings in the mail is responsible for placing all the mail in the mailbox. No exceptions.

336 When the mail enters the house, automatically place magazines and catalogs in a separate stack next to the indoor mailbox.

337 Scan the daily mail for cards or personal letters but otherwise only open mail once a week.

338 Create a simple Bill Box for paying monthly bills by using a business envelope box. Cut off the flap of box. Your folded monthly bills can stand upright in the box. Place bills in the box with your checkbook and a small solar calculator. There is no need to alphabetize bills or store under tabs since every bill in the box will be paid each month at bill paying time.

339 Once a week, deal with the mail, handling each piece only once. Each piece is *To Shred*, *To Keep*, or *To File*. You'll make 3 piles of mail accordingly. Use a letter opener to open the mail and keep a wastebasket nearby.

- **Catalogs/magazines**: Immediately recycle unwanted catalogs or magazines. Set aside the others in your *To Keep* pile.
- **Junk mail**: Open to verify that it's junk mail, then rip apart or shred since it may contain identifying personal information.
- **Bills**: Open. Immediately toss supplemental reading material if you don't plan to read it. Keep return envelope. Review the statement for accuracy. If it's accurate, tear off the bill coupon portion, insert under flap of return envelope, and place in *To Keep* pile. Place the rest in *To Shred* pile.
- **Insurance policies**. Place in *To File* pile.
- **Medical statements**. Place in *To File* pile.

- **Notes and cards.** Display in a prominent place for a couple weeks, then toss or file in a specially labeled Cards folder.
- **Invitations.** Note the day, date, time and location of the event in your day planner or phone's calendar. Display the invitation in a prominent place until event passes if desired, then toss. Another option is to file the invitation in a scrapbook file for use in creating a memory album with pictures you took at the event.
- **Weekly ads.** Peruse them for sale items to be purchased this week. Clip the needed page and put in purse or wallet. Toss the rest.

340 When the last of the mail has been opened:

- Place materials *To File* in specific labeled folders.
- Place bills *To Keep* in your Bill Box.
- Shred appropriate items.
- Place catalogs and magazines in designated reading areas—home office, bedside table, coffee table, or in your purse or briefcase to read while you're riding public transportation or waiting at the doctor's office.

341 To remove your name from direct mail lists and credit card applications go to www.dmachoice.com or www.catalogchoice.org for catalogs.

342 When you receive unsolicited requests for donations in the mail and you do not wish to make a contribution, write CANCEL on the invoice. In large script, write, "please remove my name from your mailing list." Insert the invoice in the organization's stamped self-addressed envelope and mail it back to them. It sounds harsh but it works. The organization will drop your name from its mailing list. If you prefer, call the toll-free number on the solicitation materials and ask to be removed from the organization's mailing list.

343

Keep bill paying simple by using this process:

- Create a *Bill Pay Sheet* on the computer making a table like the one shown. Make 9 columns and 20 rows. Modify the side margins of the document as needed so the page accommodates all 9 columns.
- Label each column as indicated below.
- List every monthly bill in a separate row in order of due dates, adding rows as needed.
- Continue until all regular monthly bills are listed.

Bills 2013

Due date	Bill	Amount	Jan	Feb	March	April	May	June
5th	Phone bill	$80.00						
7th	Car Insurance	$122.50 (automatic deduction)						
9th	Macy's	Pay in full each month						
15th	Visa bill	Pay in full each month						
19th	ABC Bank (car payment)	$525.00 (automatic deduction)						
20th	EFG Bank (house payment)	$1500 (automatic deduction)						

- Print the table. Punch holes in the sheet using a 3-hole punch. Place the sheet in a loose leaf 3 ring binder. Label the side binder: Bills. If the front binder cover holds a cover sheet, decorate with clip art if desired and label it Bills.

- On your *Bill Pay Sheet*, use a colored felt pen to make a division along a horizontal row, dividing your monthly bills into two equivalent amounts that equal your monthly income, *NOT* your paydays. This allows you to budget your monthly income in two increments to cover all the bills.

- Pay bills twice a month. Using a pen or pencil, write the date the bill was paid in the appropriate monthly column.

- Set up automatic payment from your checking account for as many bills as possible. Indicate *automatic* on your *Bill Pay Sheet.* At bill paying time, write the date paid and deduct amount from your checkbook.

- Pay as many bills as possible securely on-line through your bank's web site. Indicate the date paid on your *Bill Pay Sheet* and deduct from your checkbook at bill paying time.

- When an infrequent bill arrives such as payment for vehicle license tabs, write it on a blank line on your *Bill Pay Sheet* with the amount due and pay accordingly.

- Keep current and past *Bill Pay Sheets* in the same 3 ring binder. This creates a long term record of bills paid and the date paid. If needed, the bill paid date can be cross-referenced with your checkbook or bank records.

- Near the end of June, update the *Bill Pay Sheet* by listing the remaining six months of the year. Print the new sheet and insert it in the Bill binder in front of the previous sheet.

344 A file cabinet with hanging folders instead of a tabletop folder holder keeps your desktop tidier and keeps folders out of sight. Decide on file storage containers—metal cabinets, plastic bins on wheels with 2-4 drawers, or a combination of both.

345 Purchase a box of colorful or plain hanging file folders with colored or clear tabs to create folders for your specific needs. Keep the number of folders to a minimum. The more folders you have, the more papers you'll collect, the more cleaning out you'll need to do later.

Some folder ideas:

- **Current Work**: This is your immediate To Do file—paperwork for a project, meeting minutes to read, community college catalog to sign up for classes. etc. Return all To Do papers to this folder at the end of each day and pull them out the next day. This frees your desk of papers.
- **Note Pads**: A specific place to put small pads of paper for taking phone messages or jotting a quick note. Putting them in a folder keeps the desk counter clutter-free.
- **This n That**: For short term storage of papers such as your favorite basketball team's game schedule and the invitation to an upcoming wedding that has church directions and reception information. Review this file periodically and toss outdated papers.
- **Medical statements**: When the doctor bill arrives in the mail you can compare it with the medical statement to confirm your out of pocket portion.
- **Warranties:** For purchased items with a warranty, place Proof of Purchase or sales receipt in this file. Purge warranties once a year and toss warranties for products you no longer own.
- **Car insurance papers**: Shred old ones when new ones arrive.
- **Mailing lists**: Membership directory for all the clubs and organizations to which you belong. These are usually bound notebooks that won't fit in your 3 ring binder Phone Book.
- **Cards and letters received**: Birthday, anniversary and other cards received from family and friends. Go back and read the cards periodically. Eventually you'll dispose of them. If you can't part with them, place them in a labeled bin in the garage for longer term storage.
- **Catalogs**: Seed catalogs, your favorite store catalog and others from which you want to browse frequently or keep for reference. Purge once a year or as an updated catalog arrives.

- **Business files**: If you have an in-home business, keep all your business labeled folders in one file drawer. Keep your *Business Tax Deductible Expenses* folder in this drawer.
- **Owners' manuals**: Purge every few years for items you've discarded.

346 Use an accordion file folder with monthly tabs for *Personal Tax Deductible Expenses.* Place all pertinent receipts here and you'll have them all in one place at tax time. The file folder will fit in your file cabinet.

347 Create a separate accordion file folder with monthly tabs for *Business Tax Deductible Expenses.*

348 When the store clerk or restaurant wait staff hands you a credit card receipt, write *expense* on it if it's for business. Write *save* on it for a purchase that you may need to return later or if it's a credit to be applied to your credit card.

349 Place all credit card and sales receipts in a designated wallet section as you receive them. Go through your receipts once a week separating them into 4 categories:

- To toss or shred
- To file as a business receipts
- To save in an envelope for possible future return or credit
- To deduct from your checkbook as a debit purchase.

350 Keep an envelope in your Bill Box for receipts that you may need later to return or exchange a purchase. Write *Receipts* on the envelope. After a month, shred the receipts no longer needed.

351 For greeting cards use a shoe box decorated with contact paper or purchase a ready—made card box at craft or fabric stores. Make your own card dividers cut from file folders or purchase a pre-made divided box. Organize dividers by the kinds of cards most used or by alphabet.

Dividers include:

- Notes cards
- Birthday
- Anniversary
- Get Well
- Congratulations
- Baby
- Wedding
- Valentine's Day
- Easter
- Mother's Day
- Halloween
- Thanksgiving
- Thank You

352 Save time and money by purchasing greeting cards at a discount on-line from places like Current, Inc. at www.currentinc.com

353 Organize a group catalog order with colleagues at work or with your friends from card companies like Current. Oftentimes you'll receive free shipping to one address with a minimum purchase.

354 Many nonprofit organizations send greeting cards in the mail. Send them a nominal donation and file the cards in your card box.

355 If you prefer to be kinder to the environment, skip the paper cards and access one of the many on-line greeting card websites. For a small annual membership or for free, you can email electronic cards to friends and family. For added convenience, you can select the date you want the e-card sent.

356 Stockpile Christmas cards in a separate labeled box and place with the Christmas decorations. Purchase cards at after-Christmas sales and save the sets received from non-profit organizations.

357 Three-ring binders keep common themed paperwork together in one place. Sheet protectors keep papers from tearing out of the binder. Purchase binders and page protectors when school supplies go on sale.

358 Binder uses could include:

- **Phone**. Keep phone lists from your clubs, organizations, sports teams, school mailing lists, church rosters.
- **Recipes**. For loose recipes clipped from magazines and newspapers.
- **Home Decorating**. For pictures cut from design magazines of ideas you'd like to incorporate into your home.
- **Business**. For your home based business. Store handouts from training sessions, meeting minutes, invoices.
- **Health and Fitness**. Include exercises you'd like to try, nutritional information and health tips.
- **Travel**. Information on places you'd like to go, clipped from magazines and travel brochures.
- **Gardening**. Articles clipped from your favorite gardening magazines.
- **Crafts.** Instructions and pictures of crafts or sewing projects you'd like to undertake.

359 Sort magazines by category or by subscription name and store in magazine holders. Label each magazine holder. For added ease, use clip art on the label for quick category identification.

360 Digital magazine subscriptions can replace paper magazines with some publishers. Using your electronic tablet, look up your magazine subscriptions to see if the publishers offer this option. After signing up for digital service, monthly issues are automatically available on your tablet for you to download at your convenience.

361 It's more time efficient to read magazines from cover to cover rather than bounce around from article to article. Bend the corner of the page you're reading when you set it down so you'll know where to start when you pick it up again.

362 If you're planning to keep the magazine after you've read it, place an "X" on the front cover, indicating it's been read. File with others in a magazine box.

363 The benefit of paper magazines over digital ones is that you can tear out pages you want to keep. Punch holes in the pages using your 3-hole punch. File pages in appropriate 3 ring binders. Binders could include:

- Travel
- Health and Fitness
- Recipes
- Crafts/Decorating
- Other interests

364 If you're computer savvy, scan the magazine pages you want to keep and store them in folders on your computer.

365 If you're not willing to properly file the pages taken from magazines, don't tear them out. They will just become piles of clutter.

366 Various ways to recycle magazines:

- Designate a recycle box for magazines. Keep the box in a convenient location, perhaps under your desk. In addition to regular magazines, glossy ad magazines can be recycled. For more information go to www.Earth911.com

- Take magazines to work for your co-workers.
- Set up a magazine swap in the break room at work. Encourage co-workers to bring in their previously read magazines for all to enjoy.
- Drop magazines off at a retirement home or take some with you to the doctor's office.
- Take magazines to the recycling station when you do errands.

367 Build an educational reference library from your hobby magazines. Purchase a one year subscription to your favorite magazine and save each issue. After a year, you have a great reference library. At that point, discontinue the subscription. Keep no more than 12 issues of any specific magazine. It's clutter after that. Use magazine boxes to store issues. Label the boxes and store on a designated shelf.

Personal—your own things

With all our personal possessions it's a wonder we can keep track of any of them. The goal is to create places for these items, then develop the habit of putting them in their places after using them.

368 How many rings have you lost by laying them down in helter-skelter fashion anywhere and everywhere around the house? Instead, place a small, pretty glass or crystal dish on your dresser out of reach of young children. When you remove your rings for showering, housecleaning, gardening or other chores, *always* place them in the dish, no exceptions.

368 If you find yourself frequently taking rings off in the kitchen before washing dishes or doing housework, place a small glass bowl or ring holder on the window shelf as the depository. *Always* place your rings in the dish, no exceptions ever.

370 When staying away from home overnight, keep your watch and jewelry from getting lost after you remove them. Find an out of the way shelf or counter. Remove your watch and place it on the shelf or counter. When you remove your rings, place them in the circle formed by the watch. As an alternative, place your rings, watch and other jewelry in a zippered section of your purse, toiletries bag or overnight bag.

371 A woman's purse is possibly the most inconvenient place to keep car keys. Most purses are so large that one needs to dig extensively to find the keys. This creates stress and wastes both time and energy. Decide where you'll keep your keys and be religious about always putting them in their proper place after each use.

372 If you can't decide where to put your car keys and are constantly misplacing them, consider placing them into the kitchen junk drawer when you enter the house from the car. Remember to put them there after each use until you fully develop the habit.

373 Peruse garage and yard sales to find an old fashioned key holder that holds several sets of keys. Hang it on the wall in the kitchen nearest the door you exit most frequently. This is the ideal place to put your keys—car keys, a door key for when you're out walking or jogging and the RV keys.

374 Consider these other options for both men and women for storing car keys: inside a bureau drawer in the bedroom, on a small tray on top of the bureau or in a tray on the office desk. Wherever you decide to put them, use the same place and put them there every time after use.

375 Put your reading glasses away in its case before retiring for the evening.

376 Create a habit of using an eye glass cleaner and a soft cloth and clean your glasses before putting them away for the evening. You'll be rewarded with sparkling clean eyewear in the morning.

377 Have the man in your household designate a specific site for placing the items he needs to take with him each day. For example, a large tray on the corner of the kitchen counter or desk can be where he places his work name tag, security card, cell phone, car keys and any paperwork.

378 Keep your gym bag exercise-ready and in your car at all times or store your exercise gear and clothing in a rented gym locker.

379 The following items in a gym bag will get you through your swim class:

- Swim cap
- Goggles
- Swimsuit
- Beach towel
- Deodorant
- Baby powder in a small, Tupperware spice shaker container
- Flip-flops
- Gym membership card in a water tight zip lock bag
- Water bottle

380 These items in a gym bag or gym locker will get you through your workouts:

- Exercise shorts/pants and top
- Tennis shoes
- Socks
- Sports bra
- Elastic bands for tying up hair
- Deodorant
- Baby power in small shaker
- Clean pair of underwear
- Shower towel
- Shampoo in a small leak-proof bottle
- Conditioner in a small leak-proof bottle
- Small brush and comb
- Water bottle
- Gym membership card

381 After each trip to the gym, bring your bag into the house; toss the swimsuit/workout clothes/ towels in the laundry. When clothes are clean and dry, replace in gym bag. Place gym bag by the front door to take out on your next trip to the car.

382 Do you find it challenging to make time to exercise? Do exercises while watching television. Get into the habit of lifting weights or doing calisthenics during the first program you watch, or during the commercials. Keep it simple. Doing something is better than doing nothing.

383 Keep five, eight, or ten pound hand weights in the TV room. Do multiple sets of several different weight lifting exercises while watching your favorite show or during commercials. Also include the following exercises:

- Push-ups. It's okay to do the "girl" kind (knees on floor).
- Side planks
- Sit-ups
- Squats

Before you know it you'll have completed a full workout. It didn't take extra time because you were watching TV anyway.

384 It's been said that folks who exercise in the morning are more likely to stick with a fitness routine. You could set your alarm for 20 minutes earlier. Upon waking, stretch a few muscles before you get out of bed, then slide to the floor for sit-ups, push-ups and side planks. Stand and do 50 squats.

385 Keep hand weights in your bedroom. In as little as ten minutes you could do 2 sets of 8 or 9 different weight lifting exercises before you ever leave the room.

386 Use a designated notebook to record a wish list of items you'd like to purchase on a long term or short term basis. Write the items on pages according to price: less than

$100; $100-$500; $500-$1000; over $1000. By having these items written down, they become part of your subconscious. Over time you can go back and be surprised at what items you purchased.

387 Get a head start on birthdays and Christmas by shopping all year round especially for kids and grandchildren. Keep your gift purchases in a large, labeled, covered bin in the garage if there's no other place in the house for it. At gift giving time, wrap all gifts and you're done.

388 Request Christmas lists from your kids no matter their age. Keep the lists and shop from them throughout the year for birthdays, Valentine's, Easter, wedding anniversaries or other occasions for gift giving.

389 Don't get caught without a gift on short notice.

- Purchase ½ dozen small bottles of hand lotion, body wash and shower gel in various scents at Bath and Body Work's annual sale. Mix and match in a set as a gift.
- Small jar candles in various scents are always welcome gifts. Watch for sales.
- Note cards are fun to receive and fun to use and always on sale somewhere.
- Designate a bottom drawer in a chest or some other specific location for these last minute gifts. Add to your stash whenever you find these and other interesting trinkets on sale.

390 Use the notebook in your purse/messenger bag or your PDA/smartphone's memo application to write down gift ideas as they pop into your head. Listen for and write down hints dropped by family members throughout the year. For birthdays, anniversaries or Christmas you'll know just the perfect gift to purchase.

391 Set up a memo in your PDA or smart phone for information on family members. Jot down clothing and shoe sizes plus gift hints relating to their hobbies whether books, cycling, camping or backpacking gear. Since you'll usually have your PDA or smartphone with you, when you're out shopping and see a sale, you'll know what to purchase.

392 Do you misplace your car keys frequently? Instead of dropping them into your cavernous purse or setting them down who-knows-where in the house, make a new habit of placing them in the same place every time you enter the house. Potential places could be a table drawer near the door, on a tabletop tray, a dresser drawer or a key holder attached to a wall near the back door.

Purses—can't live with just one

Are you a fashionista who enjoys having a bevy of purses for different seasons, outfits or other needs? The challenge is having a system for easily moving contents from one purse to another so you'll always have what you need when you need it.

393 The best purse is a cross body bag. There's less chance that a thief will steal it from you. It keeps your hands free. You don't need to set it down to find something inside it. In addition, cross body purses come in all materials, sizes and colors.

394 Keep your purse from becoming a dumping ground. Limit the items in your purse to a functional minimum:

- Wallet
- Sunglasses in a case

- Prescription eyeglasses in a case
- Small zipper bag of loose items
- 2-3 pens
- Cell phone
- Small notepad

395 Corral those loose items in your pursue by containing them in a mesh zipper cosmetic bag. Items could include:

- travel toothbrush
- travel size toothpaste
- less than 3 oz. of hand sanitizer
- lipstick or lip gloss
- gum or breath mints
- one day supply of medications
- Imodium, gas tablets, lactose tablets or other over the counter needs
- less than 3 oz. spray bottle of eye glass cleaner
- cleaning cloth for eye glasses

396 Purchase a wallet that best accommodates the items you want to keep with you. A well-organized wallet can easily be switched from one purse to another.

397 What should you carry in your wallet? Not everything plus the kitchen sink. These are some must carry or frequently used items to carry in your wallet that if you didn't have one or another with you, that would be the day you needed it:

- Driver's license
- One major credit card
- One debit card
- Movie punch card
- Unused gift cards with balances written on them
- Library card
- Pre-paid coffee card
- Medical insurance card

- Personal business cards
- Restaurant punch cards
- Pre-paid car wash card
- Discount coupons from stores you frequent often—fabric store or department store
- Grocery store coupons

398 Consider purchasing a purse organizer. It's a one piece unit with compartments that you can lift out of one purse and insert into another.

399 If you have retail store credit cards, keep them in a secure place at home. The sales associates at the store can look up your account number with proper identification.

400 Store the account numbers for airline frequent flyer programs in your PDA or smartphone. No need to carry those cards.

401 Place all receipts in a designated section of your wallet rather than just tossing them into your purse. Once a week go through your receipts, keeping or tossing them as appropriate.

Tasks—so much to do, so little time

Do you have unfinished tasks that keep lurking in the back of your mind? Are you thinking that the list is endless and you'll never get to all of them? According to Mark Twain, the secret of getting ahead is getting started. The secret of getting started is breaking your complex overwhelming tasks into small manageable tasks, and then starting on the first one.

401 Write down *every unfinished task* no matter how long the list becomes. Break the tasks into categories (gardening, crafts, sewing, errands, administrative, etc.)

402 Keep your list of unfinished tasks in your daily *To Do* folder. You'll be surprised that once the tasks are written down they become part of your subconscious and have a way of getting done, little by little.

403 Purposefully work on one uncompleted task at a time and check it off your list. Add new tasks as they arise.

404 If you're the last one out of your bed in the morning, make it right away. Otherwise you will walk past it ten times a day or more and not take the time to make it—your mind is already on other things.

405 Teach your children from a young age to make their beds each morning.

406 Do you dislike loading or unloading the dishwasher day after day? Make a partnership with a member of the family. One unloads it when dishes are clean; the other loads it up with dirty dishes. Rotate the task among family members.

407 Partner up on clearing off the table and doing after dinner dishes. The one(s) who cook, don't have to clean up.

408 Is there an old t-shirt that needs to be tossed? Use it for the rag bag. Immediately cut off the sleeves for rags, cut the shoulders from the shoulder seam to the neck line, then cut down the center of the front and the back disassembling the whole t-shirt. Cut the large parts into small rag cloths. Take the rags to the garage and place in the plastic "rag bag" hanging from your workbench. Use rags for cleaning bicycle chains and other dirty greasy jobs, then toss.

409 Cleaning up after a party or large family gathering can be a huge task. Some folks prefer to wait until guests depart before cleaning up. In that case, do a simple preliminary clean:

- Remove dishes from table.
- Rinse beverage glasses and place on counter.
- Scrape food from plates into trash or sink disposal.
- Turn hot water faucet on.
- Layer dinnerware in the sink with water in-between each piece.

  o Layer large plates first, then salad or dessert plates, then bowls.
  o Put in cutlery (no sharp knives please).

Clean up later is quick and easy. There will be no dried-on foods stuck to the dishes. Just wipe with fresh clean warm water and put load everything into the dishwasher.

410 When's the best time to regularly clean the house or do laundry? It's a personal decision.

- Some folks prefer to dust and vacuum the house on Thursday or Friday so the house is clean for the weekend. Others conduct these chores after the weekend since everyone was home and the house needs to be straightened up, dusted and vacuumed. Decide on a specific day and stick with it as best you can.
- Washing clothes on Saturday assures that there are plenty of clean clothes for the upcoming week, especially if you have school age children. Doing laundry as needed or when the hamper is full works for others. The main thing is to be consistent, take charge of the laundry and get it done all at once for maximum time efficiency.

411 Doing the laundry can be a family affair. One adult member can sort the clothes, put them in the washer, then the dryer. Another family member can be responsible for folding all the clothes. Remember: when taking them out of the dryer, clothes must be neatly layered on top of each other to keep them wrinkle-free. NO jamming clothes into a laundry basket—ever. One exception: underwear and socks.

412 Teach your children from a young age how to help around the house on a regular basis.

- They can carry their clean, folded clothes to their bedrooms and put them in the proper drawers.
- They can clear the table of dinnerware after meals.
- Starting at age 3, little ones can put their toys away with a little guidance and assistance.

413 When it comes to household tasks, make it a family affair.

- Make a list of weekly chores.
- Divide the chores into two categories, simple—like emptying every wastebasket in the house; complex—like scrubbing the bathroom sink and toilet, or vacuuming.
- Once a week, family members take turns selecting a task from each list until all chores have been selected. Mix it up so no child does the same chore all the time.
- Collaborate on when the chores will be completed getting buy-in from each child. Let them be responsible for doing their chores within the timeframe they selected.

This n That—more helpful ideas

There are bountiful ways to save money, time, energy, space and waste on a daily basis. Figure out what works for you and stick with it. Share your ideas with your friends and family.

414 Check out the loyalty benefits at your favorite coffee shop. Starbuck's offers rewards to members who register their coffee cards on-line. After purchasing a certain number of drinks you receive a card in the mail for a free drink. In addition, after your card is registered, some ingredients are free, such as soy milk and flavorings, saving you money with every visit. You also receive a card for a free drink on your birthday.

415 Purchase a gift card for yourself at your favorite coffee shop. Use it instead of cash or a credit card for your drinks. Some companies such as Starbucks will automatically reload your card in $25 increments on-line using your credit card when your balance is low.

416 With a pre-loaded coffee card, you can wander into your favorite coffee shop without cash or having to use your credit card for your morning or afternoon coffee, latte or mocha.

417 Use leftover twist ties that come with trash bags to tie together everything from Christmas lights and tree garlands to cords of all kinds—lamps, chargers, appliances.

418 Set up a 2nd email account for entering sweepstakes and contests. This keeps your main email account void of massive marketing emails that accompany contest entries.

419 There's little or no accounting needed when you use a credit card instead of a debit card for purchases. Some simple rules:

- Use the same credit card for all your purchases.
- Budget a monthly amount for purchases.
- Keep your credit card receipts and add them up each week so you stay within your monthly budget or check your statement on-line.
- Pay off the card in full each month to not accrue interest charges.

420 You can rack up frequent flyer miles by using your credit card everywhere credit cards are accepted. Include your around town purchases over $5.00—groceries, pizza, stamps, lattes, fast food. Some companies allow credit card payment for paying utility, cable TV, insurance and phone bills. You can easily average two or three free airline tickets a year using your frequent flyer miles.

421 Your pet's gear needs a home also. Stow leashes, collars, toys and brushes in a cabinet in the utility/mud room. Keep a separate sealed small container for doggie treats from which you can grab as you head out the door with your pet.

Time Management—using time wisely

We all have the same 24 hours in a day yet others seem to get more done. The key is to be efficient with your time. Use quality shortcuts and time savers to effectively utilize your time doing projects and completing tasks.

422 Some multi-tasking is okay. Some tasks require little thinking and can be done while having a gab fest on the phone. Let your friend know you're putting her on speaker phone and complete one or more of the following:

- Make your bed
- Empty the dishwasher
- Straighten your desktop
- Straighten any room of the house
- Fold laundry
- Clean out your purse
- Organize a small drawer or section of a cupboard
- Clean the kitchen

423 Once you've looked up a phone number from the yellow pages or on your smartphone, add it to your day planner or phone Contacts. You may need the number again and will have it readily available.

424 Teach yourself to take power naps. A power nap is sleeping for 15-20 minutes and waking up feeling refreshed, energized and ready to go again.

425 How to power nap:

- Find a favorite spot in the house other than your bed for your power nap. Always nap in the same place.
- Turn on music if that soothes you.
- Set a timer for 15-20 minutes, then lie down in your favorite spot.
- Pay attention to your breathing while concentrating on the music or the silence. As you relax, your breaths will be slower, your body continues to relax and you fall sleep.
- When the timer goes off, get up and go about your business.

As your body conditions itself to sleep when you lie down in your favorite spot, you won't need a timer. You'll find that most often you automatically awake after 15-20 minutes and you feel refreshed.

426 Type up a grocery list personalized for your family. Arrange items by category such as dairy, produce, meat, baking, snack foods, etc., or arrange according to the layout of your most frequently visited grocery store. Print out several copies then save the list on your computer for future use. Keep a printed copy in the kitchen for noting weekly items to purchase.

427 Before starting any cooking or baking project fill the kitchen sink ½ full with warm, sudsy water. After using each measuring cup, gadget, bowl or cutlery, drop it in the sink to soak for easier clean up.

428 Cook once; eat twice. When you're making dinner, double the recipe. Label contents and the date, then freeze ½ batches. You can freeze, reheat and serve all in the same microwaveable Tupperware containers.

429 Cook once, eat twice ideas:

- Prepare two meatloaves. Bake one, freeze the other, uncooked.
- Cook up a double batch of spaghetti sauce.
- Make an extra-large batch of lasagna. Freeze half.
- Cook 2 pounds of ground beef with chopped onions. Use one for tacos that night; freeze the remainders in airtight Tupperware containers to use another day with spaghetti sauce from the freezer.

430 Keep the refrigerator freezer full of made ahead meals. Store extra meals and bulk items separately in a freezer in the garage. Hang a clip board with a felt pen near the garage freezer. Write down the contents of food containers in the freezer. Check off each item as you remove it from the freezer. If it's more convenient, this master list could be hung on the side of the kitchen refrigerator. Do inventory on both freezers regularly to rotate and use up the frozen food items.

431 Keep unbreakable cereal bowls and tumblers such as Tupperware in a bottom cabinet drawer or shelf within easy reach of your grade school children. With cereal in a Tupperware container and a small unbreakable container of milk and juice in the refrigerator, kids can make their own breakfast while you get a few extra winks of sleep or take your shower.

432 Fill several liquid tight Tupperware pitchers with juice or milk. Place pitchers on a lower shelf in the refrigerator so younger children can help themselves. Pitchers won't break or spill if dropped.

433 Keep your cell phone with you by day, re-charge it at night and you will never have a low battery.

434 Keep your cell phone charger in a prominent place so you won't forget to take your phone with you the next day. For example, if you place the charger with the phone on a nightstand next to your jewelry box, you can grab your watch or earrings and the phone at the same.

435 Use your cell phone's memos application as a brain dump for all those ideas and to do's that randomly pop into your head. This saves you from having scribbling on pieces of paper everywhere that easily get lost.

436 Clean out your email box as you go, deleting messages after you're read them and moving messages you want to save to folders.

437 Carry a small notebook, day planner or use your smartphone to keep track of daily tasks. Keep it with you all the time whether in your purse or messenger bag. This notebook or device contains your To Do tasks for each day. If you work from home, file your notebook in your Current Work folder at the end of each day.

438 Spend fifteen minutes each evening planning your next day. Take out your To Do List from your day planner or phone, jotting down activities, tasks or errands for the next day, or start a new list. Take fifteen minutes the next morning to review your plans and modify as needed. Planning ahead assures you don't miss an important activity or appointment.

439 If you didn't complete all the tasks on your To Do List, rewrite the remaining tasks onto a new page for a fresh focus, adding new tasks as needed. The following symbols track tasks:

> check mark—task completed
> → task moved forward to new page
> dot—task is in progress
> dot w/circle—delegated task to another, check on it
> x—task deleted

440 To keep a tighter focus on your daily To Do list, mark an * next to the task(s) that must be done that day or number your highest priority items from 1-4.

441 Small portable kitchen timers are superb time managers. You set it and forget it until it goes off. Keep several in your home and use them for keeping track of much more than what's baking in the oven. Set a timer for:

- Your nap or power nap
- The amount of time you've allotted to work on a project or specific task. When the timer rings, stop and put the project away in its proper place.
- The amount of time before your favorite TV show begins so you won't miss the opening segment.
- Outdoor water sprinklers that aren't on automatic timers.

- The 15 minutes you can continue working on your task before you need to leave to pick up the kids from school.
- The amount of time you have left before you need to get in the shower for your evening date or event.

442 These days most of us combine our errands to save time and gas. Have you ever arrived home only to realize that you forgot an errand? Use your day planner or smartphone to list the errands. Number them in order of proximity to each other. Start with #1 errand and continue until all errands are completed.

443 Take a few minutes each evening tidying up the house after dinner or after the kids are in bed. If you have organizational systems in place, this should only take a few minutes—picking up a wayward toy, book or clothing item or putting the newspaper in the recycle bin. Afterwards you can sit, relax and enjoy your evening or work on a project knowing the house is orderly. Better yet, you'll awake to a tidy house in the morning.

444 Keep your computer files simple so you can easily locate what you need. Under your computer's main hard drive such as Microsoft's My Documents, create one folder with your name: Jane. From there build sub-folders for the main topics and sub-folders under those topics as needed. Create a shortcut and pull the name folder to your desktop as an icon. Every time you start computer work you'll quickly find the documents you need by clicking on your name folder.

445 Once you return to your house from the car with your tote bag or messenger bag, take a few minutes to empty your bag. Rinse out your commuter mug and water bottle and place in dishwasher. Place loose papers in designated places or toss them. Unpack store clothing purchases, remove tags, hang or put in laundry. Store shopping bag to use again later. Place the tote bag next to your purse so it's handy to grab and go on your next outing.

446 When your reusable commuter mug and water bottle are clean from the dishwasher, immediately return them to your tote bag or messenger bag.

447 Sort mail or pay bills on-line during the commercials while watching TV.

448 Keep sale flyers and magazines in your briefcase or purse to read while riding the bus or waiting at the doctor's office.

449 To keep track of birthdays and anniversaries, set electronic reminders on your cell phone or Facebook page. As an alternative, keep a hard copy sheet of birthday and anniversaries in your Bill Box. As you pay bills, check the sheet, select a card from your Greeting Card Box, write a short note, address and stamp the envelope. Mail it with the bills. Better for your friends and family to receive a card early than to not receive one at all.

450 Always running late for an event or appointment? Use this simple method of counting time backwards to keep you or the whole family on schedule. Get out paper and pen to do the math if need be:

- What time do you need to be there? 3 PM.
- How long does it take to drive there? 30 minutes.
- How long does it take you or family members to get ready—taking a shower or changing clothes if necessary? 30-45 minutes
- Add an extra 15 minutes to get yourself or family members out the door and settled in the car with needed items.

The day of the event, announce to the family that they need to start getting ready at 1:30 and be out the door heading to the car at 2:15 PM. Set a timer to go off at 1:30 if need be. Up until 1:30, everyone can go about their business without worrying about the time.

451 When getting ready to leave the house, more times than not, one child will appear with uncombed hair, mismatched clothing or buttons askew. One parent can be responsible for overseeing one child and the other parent for the other child, or assign this task to older family members.

452 Have you oftentimes left the house without the items you needed to take with you? Perhaps you had to run around at the last minute assembling items to take? Develop a habit of gathering those items up ahead of time. Place them in your tote bag. Carry the tote bag to the door. For a morning departure, do this the night before. For an afternoon departure, do it in the morning.

453 Make it a daily routine that after homework is completed, each child returns books and paperwork to the backpack and places the backpack by the departure door. This eliminates the morning hassle of looking for both backpacks and schoolwork.

454 Is your camera prepared so you won't miss a photo opportunity? Upon arrival home after an event or trip where you took a lot of pictures, re-charge the camera. If your camera uses batteries, replace them as soon as they're low. Keep spare batteries in a small container and take it with you when you take the camera. Refill the container with batteries upon arrival home. Designate a place to put the camera so you can always locate it.

455 Was your camera's memory card full just when you wanted to take that special photo? Download digital pictures to your computer software right after each event or trip. Delete pictures from camera. Recharge the camera's battery, if needed. Camera is now fully charged and ready to go for the next event or trip.

456 Immediately after downloading the pictures from your camera to the computer, download the pictures from your computer to a CD. Label and file your digital CD's into CD albums. Label and date each album. If you're not digital savvy, ask another member of your family to take on this task for you.

457 If you're an avid photo taker, purchase CD's in a 100 pack. You'll have a ready supply of CD's every time you download pictures or want to make a photo CD as a gift.

458 Keep a mini-office in your tote bag. Keep items together in a zippered pouch. Items could include:

- Small notebook
- Kleenex
- Calculator
- Highlighter
- Pens (2)
- Permanent marker
- Mini-stapler
- Disinfectant wipes
- Hand sanitizer wipes

459 Post a large monthly calendar or one month dry erase board in the utility or family room. Designate a different color marker for each child. Write in all planned appointments/ sports practices/games and other activities for the month for each child.

Travel—oh, the places to go

Whether traveling for business or pleasure, you'll have less stress if you have travel systems in place.

460 It always takes longer to pack than one thinks. Pack the day before your trip. The next morning, you'll only need to put in last minute items such as your toiletries or cosmetic bag.

461 Since most major airlines charge for an extra bag, plan to have just one wheeled carry-on bag plus a shoulder travel tote if at all possible.

462 Lighten your travel load by leaving your everyday purse at home and using a multi-functional shoulder travel bag instead. Use the travel bag for items needed while traveling:

- Personal commuter mug
- Re-useable water bottle
- Book or magazine
- Reading glasses

463 There's no need to carry your full wallet with you while traveling since most likely you won't need all those items while out of town. Just take the more important items with you and put them in a checkbook type case in your travel bag:

- Driver's license
- One major credit card or debit card
- Medical insurance card
- Cash for food or snacks while in travel status
- Travel tickets or airline boarding pass

464 Transfer the mesh zipper cosmetic bag from your purse to your travel tote. At the airport, you can put this small bag in the security bin, as is, without having to separate liquid items. The cosmetic bag includes the same everyday items you carry in your purse:

- Travel toothbrush
- Travel size toothpaste
- Less than 3 oz. of hand sanitizer
- Lipstick or lip gloss

- Gum or breath mints
- Multi-day supply of medications
- Imodium, gas tablets, lactose tablets or other over the counter needs
- Less than 3 oz. spray bottle of eye glass cleaner
- Cleaning cloth for eye glasses
- Add:

  o ear plugs
  o disposable pre-packaged sanitizers for wiping down the airplane seat arms and beverage tray

465 Traveling light reduces your load yet assures you have essential items such as:

- Checkbook type case with ID and credit cards
- Cosmetic bag with loose items, including travel size liquids
- Cell phone
- Eyeglasses
- Sunglasses
- Book, magazine or electronic reader
- MP3 player or IPod and headphones

466 When packing for the trip home, tidy up as you pack by discarding unneeded paper items—admission receipts, travel brochures, directions, etc.

467 If you can't wash and dry dirty clothes for the trip home carry a plastic grocery bag in your suitcase for these items. Upon arrival home, empty contents of your laundry bag into the clothes hamper.

468 At home, stock a small bin with a lid with hotel shampoo, conditioners, lotions and soaps. These are less than 3 oz. and are the ideal travel size for airport security. Grab them as needed for your travel toiletries bag.

469 Consider purchasing small, liquid tight plastic bottles for travel. Save money by keeping them full of shampoo and conditioner from your larger bathroom bottles. They'll be ready to toss into your toiletry bag for your next trip.

470 Make a one-time purchase of a travel size hair spray less than 3 oz. Keep it filled with hair spray from your larger bottle and keep in your travel toiletry bag.

471 If you travel frequently, keep a travel size cosmetic bag under your bathroom sink filled with spare toiletries so you don't need to pack and unpack these items with every trip. Items could include:

- Shampoo and conditioner in refillable bottles, 3 oz. or less
- Hair spray in a refillable bottle, 3 oz. or less
- Deodorant
- Body and hand lotion
- Hair brush and comb
- Travel size toothbrush and toothpaste
- Baby powder or body dusting powder, if used, in a small Tupperware spice shaker
- Facial wipes for removing makeup
- Headband to keep hair away from your face when washing or applying makeup

472 Always place bottles containing liquids in a zip-lock bag to protect your clothing and other items from leaks or spills. If these items are in your carry-on bag, you can place the whole bag in the bin when passing through security.

473 If you travel frequently to a vacation home or to visit adult kids, keep a permanent supply of everyday toiletries in a travel bag at that location. This enables you to travel lighter, gets you through airport security faster with a minimum of or no liquid items. If visiting relatives, ask where you can store the bag so it won't be in their way.

474 By keeping spare toiletries at a location you visit frequently, you are not limited to taking travel size bottles or supplies. When you arrive at your destination, purchase larger bottles of shampoo, conditioner, hairspray, facial cleanser, body lotion, bath powder or other everyday items. Stash them in your travel bag and tuck the bag out of sight in a location designated by the hosts.

475 If you travel frequently and there's an item always lacking where you stay, take one with you if possible. Many home bathrooms do not have a guest water tumbler for taking medications so consider carrying your own plastic one in your toiletries bag. Or if you keep items at a family member's home, add the plastic tumbler to your stashed bag.

476 If you work out frequently when visiting your adult kids, store tennis shoes and workout clothes at their house to avoid packing these for each trip.

477 A classic picnic basket is good for much more than picnics in the park near home. Take it with you to kids' sports activities filled with snacks or lunch. Take it with you in the car on road trips. Until you reach your destination you can make stops at grocery stores for fruit and ready-made foods. Take a cooler full of beverages, including milk, and fixings for sandwiches or salads. Use Tupperware containers for cereal. Keep everything in your picnic basket for eating breakfast in your hotel room when continental breakfasts are not available. The family can eat lunch at a rest area or city park. This allows the family to eat more healthfully and for less money.

478 Purchase a picnic basket from the thrift store or at a yard sale. Store the picnic basket in the house where you can get at it when needed. With this to-go basket, a hotel room quickly becomes a mini-kitchen. Keep it stocked with the following items:

- Be kind to the environment by using re-useable, unbreakable Tupperware plates, bowls and tumblers, one for each family member
- Metal fork, knife and spoon for each person
- Two metal serving spoons
- Cloth napkins, one per person, or paper napkins
- Small cloth or vinyl tablecloth
- A manual can opener
- Small cutting board
- A utility knife
- Liquid-tight container with a squeeze cap, filled with dish soap
- 2 kitchen microfiber dishtowels and washcloths
- Several medium size liquid and air tight Tupperware storage containers
- Zip lock bags for miscellaneous food storage
- Paper towels to use for clean ups and spills
- Plastic grocery bags for storing dirty dishes and utensils until they can be washed.

479 Tupperware storage containers with virtually liquid-tight and air-tight seals keep leftovers from the restaurant fresh. Put leftovers in the car cooler or the hotel refrigerator to eat later.

480 A laundry basket or an old-fashioned milk crate in the car can hold Tupperware containers full of cookies, potato chips, cut up fruit and vegetables and other snacks.